DUELING EAGLES
Reinterpreting The U.S.- Mexican War, 1846-1848

DUELING EAGLES

Reinterpreting
The U.S.- Mexican War,
1846-1848

EDITED BY
RICHARD V. FRANCAVIGLIA
AND DOUGLAS W. RICHMOND

Texas Christian University Press
Fort Worth

Library of Congress Cataloging-in-Publication Data

Dueling eagles: reinterpreting the U.S.-Mexican War, 1846-1848 /
edited by Richard V. Francaviglia and Douglas W. Richmond
    p.cm.
    Selected papers from a symposium held at the University of
Texas at Arlington, Oct. 25-26, 1996.
    Includes bibliographic references and index.
    ISBN 0-87565-232-8 (alk. Paper)
    1. Mexican War, 1846-1848. I. Francaviglia, Richard V. II.
Richmond, Douglas W., 1946-

E415.D84 2000
973.6'2—dc21

00-034337

Design by Shadetree Studio

Contents

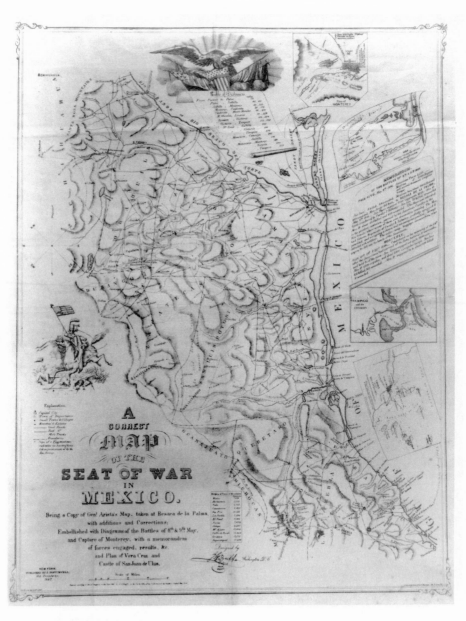

A Correct Map of the Seat of War in Mexico. Philadelphia: J. Disturnell, 1847.
(Cartographic History Library, Special Collections Division, The University of Texas at
Arlington Libraries, Arlington, Texas.)

Introduction

On October 25 and 26, 1996, the University of Texas at Arlington hosted a symposium marking the sesquicentennial of the beginning of the U.S.-Mexican War. Lasting from 1846 to 1848, the war permanently affected the relationship between the two countries.

As stated in the symposium literature, our goal was not to celebrate or glorify the conflict, but to look back upon it from 150 years of historical perspective. We attempted to view the war dispassionately, but soon realized that the war is still capable of generating much passion. The symposium, which was jointly sponsored by the National Park Service as part of their annual Palo Alto Conference, thus endeavored to promote a better understanding of the war's significance and its impact upon the people who live along both sides of today's border. The symposium focussed on the social history of the war because we felt that it had been neglected. Although scholars over the years have made great strides in interpreting the U.S.-Mexican War, much of their emphasis has been on the military aspects of this conflict. Thus, the international group of speakers at the meeting spent much time emphasizing the social and cultural effects of the conflict in addition to the more traditional themes.

The articles in this anthology represent selected papers from the symposium. The studies herein attempt to shed light on previously obscure themes. They reveal that the U.S.-Mexican War remains an unplowed field in many respects, and the scholars who came to

Arlington have whetted the appetite for new interpretations. Approximately 170 people attended and many of them asked the presenters for additional information; others who attended absorbed the ideas they heard quietly but they, too, learned about the most dramatic episode in U.S.-Mexican relations.

We have rearranged the papers in this book so that they first introduce the reader to the subject on a geographical basis, then explore in detail that which has often been overlooked. To help readers better envision the immense size of areas affected by the war, Richard Francaviglia begins by analyzing the historical and geographical factors that affected both operations and broader political developments associated with the war. Francaviglia reveals the stunning geographic panorama of the borderlands in the mid-nineteenth century, and how the physical landscape not only affected the movements of armies but also helped shape national identities. Francaviglia concludes that one major outcome of the war, the border, was a true intercultural frontier rather than a demarcated barrier. Just as the Río Grande, or Río Bravo del Norte, often changes course so, too, has the border between the United States and Mexico during the nineteenth century. The cartographic materials that help illustrate Francaviglia's article demonstrate the changing knowledge of and agreement concerning the border throughout a critical period in United States and Mexican history.

Once readers understand the geography of the war, they are better prepared to understand how its history has been shaped by the conflict. We felt that the underlying causes of the war needed to be considered and interpreted from the perspectives of both Mexico and the United States. While the basic causes of the war are fairly well known, the complexicities that also propelled the conflict into taking place are the subject of the initial essays. Professor Sam Haynes discusses the United States' motivation for the war in the context of U.S.-British relations. Here it becomes clear that the struggle engaged British and French diplomats who were eager to check U.S. expansionism. The problem was that Mexico had a difficult time recognizing its loss of Texas. Mexico continued to insist that the boundary between it and the Texas Republic was the Nueces River and not the Río Grande. Britain offered to guarantee Mexico's northern border largely by means of her independent-minded representative in Texas. Slippery diplomatic maneuvers only raised the fears of many U.S. citizens. Indeed, Haynes contends that anti-British sentiment, largely owing to a belief that Britain intended to seize Mexican lands, became an underlying factor in shaping the sentiments of Manifest Destiny that circulated throughout the 1840s.

One of Mexico's most renowned historians and undoubtedly the leading expert on the U.S.-Mexico War, Josefina Zoraida Vázquez, interprets the causes of the war within the context of a comprehensive domestic and international framework. Mexico's inability to colonize its northern frontier resulted in a lack of population in the regions sought by President James Polk. Although the United States was hardly a bastion of political stability at the time, neither was Mexico: that young nation suffered from a fierce dispute between federalists, who wanted self-rule as much as possible, centralists, who felt that a strong central state was the best course for Mexico to follow, and moderates who sought to compromise. Here even Spain became involved in the partisan struggles by attempting to place a Spanish prince on a Mexican throne. The British and French supported this monarchist scheme quietly before abandoning Mexico just as the war broke out. Yet political sectarianism continued; the national government had to send out troops to crush domestic revolts as U.S. forces fought with Mexican soldiers in the north. The war became a tragedy for Mexico because her institutions failed at a critical time when President James K. Polk was determined to seize the Southwest, either by purchase or by provoking armed conflict. Why Mexico lost the war is an elusive theme, which other authors have confronted.

A symposium analyzing a war cannot overlook military perspectives so the organizers called upon Bruce Winders, whose essay revolves around the behavior of volunteers and the problems they presented when challenging an unpopular officer. Ever since the colonial period, the United States had depended upon a militia system based upon techniques developed in the days of Oliver Cromwell.

Even though they were not always effective, militias continued to be the basis for U.S. land forces largely because of the minuteman legend and the fear of standing armies. Although the United States had learned much about military organization from the War of 1812, the war between Mexico and the United States demonstrated finally that professional army units would become the only sensible future. Even in the U.S.-Mexican War, however, the often disruptive presence of volunteers was palpable: As Winders demonstrates in his essay on the Paine Mutiny, headstrong volunteers caused a good deal of friction within the U.S. military.

It is probably fair to state that the evening address by Miguel González of the Universidad Autónoma de Nuevo León moved the participants more than any other presentation. His discussion of the difficulties faced by the citizens of Monterrey is quite compelling. One learns that the pain of occupation under U.S. forces affected Mexicans throughout the northeast in many ways that are still felt today. The horror of war is never pleasant, particularly when it harms innocent civilians.

Mitchel Roth emphasizes a major innovation of the period—the advent of modern war correspondence. Here the efforts of journalists demonstrate the insatiable appetite for news in the United States about its war with Mexico. Roth describes the technological advances that often enabled newspaper readers to receive dispatches covering major events before the secretary of war learned about them. During the war, the popular press came into its own and, like today's media coverage of modern issues, had a great effect on the way in which the public perceived the conflict. Although reporters portrayed Mexico as a weaker nation than the United States, Mexico fascinated U.S. readers. The proximity of Mexico made it an accessible landscape for high adventure, and the war provided the justification for young males to volunteer their services. Reports about the battles read like Gothic drama, and the Mexican people became an object of curiosity among the general public.

The regional dimensions of the conflict reveal the weaknesses that prevented Mexico from responding more forcefully. Douglas W.

Richmond describes the various problems the Mexican government experienced in dealing with its southeastern and far northern posses- sions. Clearly the demand for autonomy was uppermost in the minds of those Mexicans farthest from Mexico City. But ethnic problems regarding the treatment of indigenous peoples and the desire for trade with Europe and the United States also motivated rebellion. Therefore collaboration often made it easier for U.S. forces to occupy critical areas of Mexico in Yucatán and in northern Mexico with lit- tle or no resistance. A caste dimension clearly emerges because most of the elite did not oppose U.S. forces while the guerrillas often received mass support.

In the United States, opinions about the war also showed a strong regional bias. The northeast became the bastion of anti-war senti- ment while the south and west supported Polk. This regional divi- siveness contributed in some degree to the American Civil War. It can certainly be argued that the war between Mexico and the United States provoked civil wars in both countries, since the 1858-1860 civil war in Mexico emanated from the desire of the liberal faction to eradicate the privileges of the church and military, whom they con- sidered negligent in their loyalty and ability to defend Mexico.

Intellectuals in the United States responded passionately to the war with Mexico. Professor Robert W. Johannsen describes eloquent- ly how the fighting fit into the broader pattern of U.S. attitudes— both among the country's intellectual elite, as well as in the popular culture. Even egalitarians like Walt Whitman and Robert Longfellow considered the early triumphs of the U.S. military as a vindication of republican virtues over medieval, Hispanic traditions. Whitman sup- ported the Democratic administration staunchly, convinced that the party was representative of the U.S. public. Whitman believed that because the public had elected Polk, the will of the people had become public. Whitman's strong support of the war began to wane, however, as he lost faith in the Democratic leadership and he saw the war in moral, rather than purely political, terms. And yet the idea that the lives of all peoples would be improved by the policies pursued in the name of republicanism by the United States prevailed in many of the pro-war writings. Because the exuberant confidence of the Jacksonian period had not ebbed away, Robert Johannsen's discussion of the literary response of U.S. thinkers captures the spirit of the times by emphasizing the generally positive reaction of the intellectuals.

Nevertheless, as Johannsen demonstrates, several literary luminaries—including Ralph Waldo Emerson and Henry David Thoreau—criticized the war eloquently. None of their anti-war writings, however, could stop the forces of war nor convince most U.S. citizens that the conflict was immoral. Because Emerson did most of his writing about the confict in journals, his opinions did not reach the general public. Furthermore, a circle of colleagues sharing Emerson's views often felt that to speak publicly against the war would be either mistaken or futile because it was unable to convince the public that the war was unjust. Slavery was at the heart of the transcendentalist argument against the fighting, because abolitionists recognized that the outcome of the war would determine the future direction of democratic principles.

This, then, is a binational re-interpretation of important, but overlooked aspects of the U.S.-Mexican War. If , as our presenters hoped, these essays help shed new light on this pivotal historic event, then our purpose will have been served.

* * *

In addition to the scholars who made presentations and prepared essays, several people and institutions deserve to be acknowledged for their support of this endeavor. Several commentators at the conference, particularly Peggy Cashion, Don Coerver, Pedro Santoni and Paul Vanderwood, provided stimulating insights while effectively improving the quality of these essays. The Summerlee Foundation of Dallas provided funding for the symposium, as did the Texas Committee for the Humanities, and the *Arlington Star-Telegram*. The University of Texas at Arlington's Center for Greater Southwestern Studies and the History of Cartography and the Palo Alto Battlefield National Historic Site, as well as the Special Collections Division of the University of Texas at Arlington Library, sponsored the sympo-sium. Kit Goodwin coordinated the transfer of illustrative materials to editor Tracy Row, who attented the symposium and skillfully managed the publication of this book. Lois Lettini and Darlene McAllister, administrative secretaries at the Center for Greater Southwestern Studies and the History of Cartography, helped organize many details and typed numerous drafts of this manuscript in preparation for pub-lication. More recently, the center's administrative secretary Linda Julien helped orchestrate the proofreading of galley copies by the authors. As always, the UTA History Drpartment strongly supported this publication.

Douglas W. Richmond
Professor of History

Richard V. Francaviglia
Director, Center for Southwestern
Studies and Professor of History

1.
The Geographic and Cartographic Legacy of the U.S.-Mexican War

Richard V. Francaviglia

The United States-Mexican War of 1846-1848 is traditionally interpreted in historic terms, but it can also be explored in geographic and cartographic context. This spatial perspective is appropriate, for the war itself was fought on a huge and incredibly diverse geographic stage consisting of almost half of the entire North American continent. The war and the territory it involved was portrayed in a wide range of maps, both military and commercial. The U.S.-Mexican War, in fact, may be among the first of the "modern" conflicts in that so many people became cognizant of the changing geopolitical fortunes of both countries through a series of rapidly produced and distributed maps. These maps were printed in numerous venues, but newspapers and flyers were commonly used to distribute their cartographic information to readers throughout the United States.

It should be remembered that at the beginning of the nineteenth century, Mexico covered more than one-third of the entire North American continent, extending as far northwest as the present California-Oregon border at 42° north latitude and northeast to the Missouri River. The 1803 Louisiana Purchase had reduced considerably the northeastern frontier of what was once New Spain. By 1819, the Adams-Onís Treaty had established along the Sabine, Red and Arkansas Rivers, a boundary between Spain and the United States that would prove to be tenuous. Dr. John H. Robinson's *A Map of Mexico, Louisiana, and the Missouri Territory* (1819) reveals a tenuous border between northern New Spain and the United States. As David Weber and other historians have shown, the boundary would rapidly change due to two major geopolitical realities: (1) the creation of the independent Republic of Mexico in 1821; (2) the irrepressible west-ward move of European Americans, to whom treaties (either with Native Americans or even other countries such as Britain and Mexico) meant little. As a result of Texas independence (1836) and that republic's subsequent annexation to the United States (1845), Mexico's northeastern border had been substantially reduced. Mexico claimed the Nueces River as the border, but the Río Grande (or Río Bravo del Norte as it was known in Mexico) was claimed by Texas and the United States as the border.

To U.S. expansionists, northern Mexico seemed to be blocking the natural course of empire inasmuch as it lay athwart possible trade routes to the Pacific. Rebellions in California in the early 1840s reflected a rising tide of anti-Mexican sentiment in that province as European Americans established themselves on the Pacific Coast. Growing tension with Mexico also promised, or rather threatened, to bring Britain into the picture, a clearly undesirable situation that fed the fuel of Anglophobia. Thus, on the eve of the U.S.-Mexican War in the middle 1840s, Mexico's northern frontier was disintegrating under the pressure of Anglo-American intrusion and the internal dif-ficulties faced by Mexico in managing this distant northern frontier from Mexico City.[1]

The remainder of Mexico stretched southward well into the trop-ics—its southernmost tip being about 14° north of the Equator. South of the disputed rivers at the Texas border, the Gulf of Mexico defined the eastern margins of Mexico. To the west, the Pacific Ocean defined the country. Strategically speaking, Mexico was a huge, geographical-ly diverse, funnel-shaped country. That configuration had long drawn the interest of expansionist-minded *norteamericanos*, who realized that the Isthmus of Tehauntepec was in a strategic position to permit trade from the Atlantic to the Pacific, thus helping to open trade with Asia. They also observed that Mexico was essentially bounded by water on its eastern and western flanks—a condition that made it vulnerable

Map of Mexico, Louisiana, and the Missouri Territory (1819) by Dr. John H. Robinson.
(Special Collections Division, The University of Texas at Arlington Libraries, Arlington,
Texas.)

to attacks from the sea. This was particularly distressing to Mexican observers who lamented the country's relatively small navy.

Even in terms of terrestrial forces, Mexico's northern border was difficult to defend because it was rather sparsely settled and isolated from Mexico's major centers of population and political power. Because Mexico's northern frontier with the United States occupied a generally arid to semi-arid land of relatively light population density, it was theoretically easy to penetrate by invading troops who would not face well-defended and well-fortified population centers. The region's aridity, however, made invasion in the north difficult. Yet, because those areas of northeastern Mexico could be reached by sea, and because the U.S. could amass ground troops near the mouth of the Río Grande, it is not surprising that the war started there. In this action, Mexico claimed that it was simply defending its sovereign territory. The United States made a similar claim—that Mexican troops had shed U.S. blood on U.S. soil. That claim had a disingenuous ring to objective observers, but sounded reasonable to those who commonly held expansionist sentiments.

Geographers at the time were well aware of the varied landscapes and climates of the large expanse of Mexico into which U.S. troops, inexperienced in fighting within heavily mountainous, tropical or subtropical areas, would advance. Then, too, the conflict would offer the United States its first encounter with desert warfare. Stretching from the tropics to the mid-latitudes and featuring highly diverse topography (from mountains of 18,700 feet near Mexico City and areas below sea level in the California deserts), Mexico is extremely varied geographically. Because the country extends for so great a distance latitudinally and is topographically complex, its climate is quite wide-ranging, a point frequently commented on by contemporary observers at the dawn of the war. For example, the northern and more elevated portions of Mexico in the vicinity of the city of Santa Fe, New Mexico, is noted by residents and travelers to feature large, seasonal temperature variations and extreme winter cold. Yet, the southern and lowland reaches of the country in the vicinity of Tampico or Mazatlán are decidedly tropical. It was this varied environment, and the flourishing micro-organisms that inhabited it, that would prove more vexing to United States troops than the actual warfare itself.

In interpreting the U.S.-Mexican War, one should not underestimate the considerable geographical information that had accumulated over the years and now clearly served as "intelligence." In the early 1800s, the entire area of New Spain (and later Mexico) was brilliantly mapped by German scientist Alexander von Humboldt and U.S. entrepreneurial explorer Zebulon Pike. Pike's map (said to be based on von Humboldt's) was widely circulated and no doubt helped fuel visions of Manifest Destiny. Politicians often consulted maps that had been prepared for other purposes, even scientific, as the relationship between von Humboldt and Pike suggest.

Scientists of the era, both Mexican and North American, suspected that the climatic variations in Mexico were in part a result of topography, global and regional air masses, and resulting weather patterns. Whereas the prevailing tradewinds blow from the Gulf toward tropical Mexico in the vicinity of Veracruz, especially in July when they are most noticeable, westerly winds prevail in the northern reaches. Correlated with both elevation and latitude, precipitation varies from the humid tropical lowlands (which are characterized by wet summers, fairly dry winters, and rather dense jungle growth), to the mild coast of California, with its characteristically benign but often wet winters and dry summers typical of "Mediterranean" climates elsewhere. Between the tropics and the mid-latitudes there lies an extensive area of elevated basins and tablelands characterized by prolonged drought; most of this interior upland area possesses dry winters and hot summers that are occasionally mitigated by spotty afternoon thundershowers as moisture finds its way inland from either the Gulf of California or the Gulf of Mexico.

It was this large, climatically and physiographically diverse country that U.S. troops penetrated in 1846 and 1847, and that Mexican troops sought to defend against what the Mexicans viewed as a clearly unwarranted and even imperialistic invasion. So widespread were the hostilities in this war, and so distinctive the geography, that it can be said that virtually every battle has come to be characterized by the geographic

environments either encountered there by U.S. troops or defended by
the Mexican forces. For example, the Brazito Battlefield, in today's
southern New Mexico, was defined by the arm of the Río Grande and
its thickly vegetated, low-lying, marshy countenance.[2] As illustrated in
the flourishing military reports, maps, and correspondence of the period, five major environments can be discerned:

The Eastern Coastal Lowlands which, in the Veracruz vicinity of
southeastern Mexico, are situated on a coastal shelf at the base of
mountains. This exemplifies the conditions encountered along the
tropical coast with its high humidity and heavy precipitation, especially in the summer. To the north, the Gulf's subtropical lowlands
widen in the vicinity of Corpus Christi, Texas. As suggested above, it
was this area that witnessed the build-up of troops in May of 1846 and
provided many U.S. soldiers their first experience with the rather des-
olate, semi-arid Mexican countryside. Here the troops under General
Zachary Taylor first praised the invigorating onshore summer breezes,
or "tradewinds" as they were erroneously called, but by late fall cursed
the frequent "northers" that brought cold temperatures and rain.
These erratic weather conditions helped to debilitate the troops as
microbiological diseases began to take their toll. The battlefronts
along the lower Río Grande Valley in the vicinity of Resaca de la
Palma were adjacent to the coast and had a similar climate. Here,
standing water contributed to its "miasmatic" reputation. Although
the cause was not known, the disease was in fact attributable not to
the swamps themselves, but rather to the mosquitoes that bred so
readily there. The entire eastern coastline of Mexico possessed a
broad coastal shelf and shallow waters that extended for a considerable distance offshore. This made military penetration somewhat
more difficult as submerged bars could ground vessels seeking to move
through the passes (or inlets). In southern Mexico, too, yellow fever
could be added to the list of hazards facing troops. Thus sanitation—
always a problem in military operations—was in part exacerbated by
weather conditions.

* * *

The Central Plateaus and Interior Mountains. Troops entering Mexico in the vicinity of Monterrey and Buena Vista ascended into an arid, starkly mountainous country. This is a vast area of mountain ranges whose bases are buried in deep alluvial valleys. The drier or more interior of these valleys drain into dry lakes, or *playas*. The area included relatively isolated cities, such as Chihuahua and Saltillo. It is a striking, even austere region of elevated topography that would be penetrated on several fronts but only with great difficulty; for example, Colonel Alexander Doniphan's daring and exhausting troop movements into central Mexico traversed broad desert-like basins (or *bolsónes*) that were punctuated by rugged mountains. The high mountains ran north-south like corrugated ribs through the countryside and influenced the war by making troop travel exceedingly difficult. The topography, especially passes where troops could advance, provided a crucial factor in warfare. General Zachary Taylor was aware, for instance, that there were only two passes through the Sierra Madre Oriental, and that controlling these passes meant occupying northeastern and northern Mexico; hence his attack on Monterrey. During the Battle of Buena Vista, the inability of the Mexican army to move artillery into place was in part determined by the topography. Farther west, in what is today southern Arizona, the Mormon Battalion traversed the basin and range country in the vicinity of the San Pedro River. Here they encountered wild bulls and were aware of the constant threat of Apache Indians. It should be remembered that the Mormons actually began to settle the Great Basin at the very time (1847) that the area was still nominally Mexican territory. The Mormon Battalion, in fact, helped the Latter-day Saints gain a better understanding of the region's geography and potential for settlement. Here they hoped to create a theocratic empire called "Deseret."

Beyond the Rockies, John Frémont and others explored the formidable Great Basin on their way to California. The Great Basin, a stark region of interior drainage had been reconnoitered a generation earlier by the mountain men, but it was mostly avoided due to the harshness of conditions and its desert-like demeanor. Subsequent exploration would reveal that a large portion of northwestern Mexico was physiographically part of the "basin and range" (*bolsón y montaña*) region, which today includes portions of the desert states of Sonora, Chihuahua, Utah, Nevada and Arizona. The interior drainage character of the Great Basin portion of the intermountain West (most of Nevada and the western half of Utah) was so enigmatic that explorers only figured it out on the eve of the U.S.-Mexican War.

The Volcanic Highland Region (or the Sierra Volcánica Transversal), in which is located the country's—and North America's—largest single population center, Mexico City. Here the soil is fairly rich, the climate mild, and the water sources dependable. These conditions have helped sustain agriculture and a large, densely settled population since prehistoric times. In the southern reaches of the volcanic highlands, General Antonio López de Santa Anna's troops attempted to repel General Winfield Scott's advance in ferocious hand-to-hand combat at the strategic battle of Cerro Gordo. Once the hill at Cerro Gordo fell to advancing U.S. troops, Scott cleared the way for his march into Mexico City in April 1847. It was here, in the valley of Mexico, that important battles such as Contreras, Churubusco, El Molino del Rey and Chapultepec were fought. Many of the battles were illustrated by war correspondents, and this helped bring the exotic landscapes of Central Mexico into the consciousness of readers in the United States. Rimmed by tall volcanoes, the Valley of Mexico is situated high (about 7800 feet or 2600 meters) above sea level. Given its upland subtropical location, the climate here is mild despite the altitude. When in the Valley of Mexico, U.S. troops found well-watered areas, and the topography made for relatively easy movement —except in areas of volcanic flows. To reach the valley from the eastern coastal lowlands, however, invading troops had to ascend the precipitous eastern face of the sierra.

Coastal California. Stretching from Alta California far south into Baja California for nearly 2000 miles, this coastline is shoe-horned between mountainous topography and the sometimes stormy Pacific

Ocean. Although narrow, the California coast was accessible to maritime troop movements. The numerous harbors in the richest and most populous part of the coast, Alta California, provided easy entry for naval forces such as those under the command of John D. Sloat and Robert F. Stockton. Weather conditions, however (including strong winds and fog), often made for rough going. This coastal portion of California, especially Alta California, was fairly well-populated, having been settled by means of a series of Spanish and, later, Mexican missions. Tellingly, most of the population centers that were captured were close to the sea, for California's interior valleys were less densely populated by Indian peoples, and hence less attractive to Spanish and Mexican settlement. Baja California, although more lightly populated than the north, was also invaded by the sea as most of its settlements of any consequence (La Paz, for example) were coastal ports.

The Western Great Plains. Although not part of the military campaign, the plains of extreme northeastern Mexico (present-day eastern Colorado, New Mexico, and the Texas-Oklahoma panhandle) became important for U.S. troop movements. Nominally part of the land ceded during the Louisiana Purchase but still eyed with concern by Mexico, it was this vast tract on Mexico's northeastern frontier that had been a strategic gateway into northern Mexico since the 1700s. At the time of the U.S.-Mexican War, the region had earned the name "Great American Desert," though in fact much of the area was covered by short prairie grasses. On this front, too, Mexico proved vulnerable as troops could move deeper into the country from the east by traversing the longitudinal river valleys that provided water, wood and shelter, as witnessed by the invasion of Santa Fe by soldiers under the command of Stephen Watts Kearny.

So dominant is the topography and physiography of Mexico that it had to be taken into account to achieve success or avoid disaster. For example, because the coast in the vicinity of Texas was particularly difficult for maritime operations due to its shallowness, special

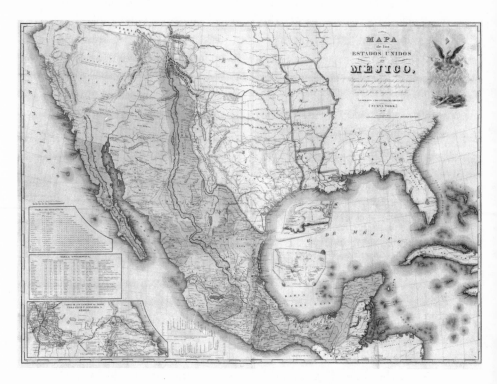

Map by J. Disturnell served as the treaty map at the end of the U.S.-Mexican War. (Cartographic History Library, Special Collections Division, The University of Texas at Arlington Libraries, Arlington, Texas.)

vessels with shallow drafts had to be acquired for operations there. Potable water, too, was so difficult to find that, on several occasions, vessels had to return all the way to Pensacola, Florida, from the Gulf coast to replenish supplies. It should be restated that although the U.S.-Mexican War was largely terrestrial in nature, most of the American troops entered the fray by sea, while most of their Mexican counterparts were land based. This further underscores the reputation of the war in Mexico as an invasion.

After their maritime transport, U.S. troops advancing into the various areas of Mexico also conducted terrestrial reconnaissance operations. These helped chart the countryside for future settlement and development which, it was widely believed, would inevitably occur after the war had been won. Noteworthy in this regard are the explorations of the steamboat *Major Brown*, which ventured far up the Río Grande on an ostensibly military reconnaissance until reaching rapids beyond Laredo; the expedition continued overland to Presidio, where its chronicler Bryant Tilden carefully noted the prospects for settling the countryside.[3] Thus it could be said that even as the fighting raged, but especially during lulls in the action, U.S. troops and their leaders viewed the Mexican landscape with an eye toward its prospects as United States territory.

How did the United States gain such detailed information about the Mexican countryside? Historian Jack Jackson suggests that some of it came from the Mexicans themselves. Using General Taylor's "astonishing" map of northeastern Mexico as an example, Jackson observed that an 1840 map by José Sánchez was seized from General Mariano Arista in the battles of Palo Alto and Resaca de la Palma.[4] This and other maps enabled the U.S. military to gain strategic information about sources of water, as well as roads and settlements. The information on these military maps was incorporated into popular maps of the period. On the U.S. side of the border, they strengthened a desire to own what would be taken from Mexico. Jackson further observes that the maps also helped Mexico better understand its northern frontier at the close of the war.

At the conclusion of the war in 1848, Mexico ceded approximately one-half of its territory to the United States. This amounted to about a million square miles and represented a significant re-orientation of Mexico's northern frontier. The Treaty of Guadalupe Hidalgo ostensibly protected the rights of former Mexican citizens who now found themselves citizens of the United States. However, state and territorial governments devised various methods to separate former residents of Mexico from their land in what was now the United States. But United States citizenship did, in some cases, provide haven or asylum to some former Mexican citizens. For example, a large group of Baja Californians had supported the U.S. during the war, and upon the establishment of the current border were permitted to relocate to Alta California for fear of retribution or retaliation.[5]

The border, or *la frontera*, was formally established along the Río Grande to Paso del Norte and thence roughly in a line due west to the Gila River, then to the west coast. This line, as agreed upon at the Treaty of Guadalupe Hidalgo, in effect cut across the grain of the countryside from the coastal subtropical lowlands of Texas to the Pacific coastal lowlands in the vicinity of San Diego, California. The border was inaccurate due to errors in surveying and reconnaissance that were included in the Disturnell treaty map, however, and the rather inaccurate subsequent surveys of John Russell Bartlett—who was empowered by his Whig acquaintances serving in Congress. Critics have noted that Bartlett lacked experience despite his talents as an artist and writer, and it has been suggested that his ultimate goal was to produce a travel book on the region. In his survey, Bartlett was aided by Andrew B. Gray of Texas, who one historian characterized as a mediocre surveyor motivated by an allegiance to southern railroad interests bent on reaching the Pacific.

Thus it was that the border's initial location was flawed from the outset. Bartlett's amiably agreeing on a borderline with Mexican General Pedro García Condé—a line some thirty miles north (that is into the U.S.) from where most American observers knew it should be—prompted United States outrage in 1851. The fracas precipitated the involvement of the more competent William H. Emory, whose efforts resulted in the increasingly accurate surveying and mapping of the border. Research by Paula Rebert notes that accurate maps of the U.S.-Mexican borderlands were the result of jointly appointed survey teams. Rebert has perceptively noted that greater geographic error resulted when the U.S. and Mexican teams worked separately than when they worked cooperatively—a harbinger of a truism along the border, namely, that the most effective policies are internationally integrated rather than separate ventures.[6]

During the early 1850s, the embarrassing realization that the Gila River did not represent the most feasible transcontinental railroad route precipitated another international crisis that the 1854 Gadsden Treaty and Purchase (or Treaty of La Mesilla as it is called in Mexico) resolved. This agreement positioned the border in its present location considerably south of the Gila River. Tucson is located in this large area, or "strip," that constitutes the southern portion of today's states of Arizona and New Mexico. By the early 1850s, then, what was at first a somewhat vague treaty boundary soon became an important zone of contact between the United States and Mexico, the *frontera internacional*, or more broadly the "Borderlands." This line stretches along the Río Grande to El Paso, thence westward along southern New Mexico and Arizona, thence to the coast just south of San Diego, where it divides Alta and Baja California politically. The border has never been as rigid in reality as it is on maps, for it is somewhat permeable to human aspirations and commercial as well as criminal forces.

Geographically speaking, a major consequence of the U.S.-Mexican War was that the United States now had a rather well-defined "Southwest" that reached to the Pacific as an outcome of the Manifest Destiny sentiments that had been voiced well before the war.[7] As a consequence, Mexico found itself with an arid and rather mountainous northern frontier, or *el norte*, which is still a developing zone today. Mexico's northern frontier has had a powerful effect on the country's economy and psyche, but, as noted by historian David Weber, *el norte* does not appear to be celebrated in myth south of the border quite as enthusiastically as European Americans have romanticized their southwestern frontier.[8]

The substantive differences between economies and political philosophies between these two great countries have led to disparities and dissimilarities along the border and continue to lead to speculation about what might have happened if the war had never occurred: consider today's Tucson as a Sonoran rather than an Arizonan city; or the character of say, Hermosillo, if the United States had claimed even more territory as an outcome of the war. Until the development of NAFTA, the pace of economic development was less intense on the Mexican side of the border, but today the rapid pace of change, growth and migration gives U.S. cities along the border area a decidedly hispanic quality, while their counterparts in Mexico have become somewhat more "western" in design, appearance, and economy.

North of the border, one still hears claims that the U.S. might have taken even more of Mexico than it had during the war. This, however, is doubtful and not for reasons of U.S. compassion: in reality, the United States probably would not have been able to hold much more territory than agreed upon in the Treaty of Guadalupe Hidalgo as considerable guerrilla warfare was endemic and had taken its toll on U.S. troops. Also, solid enough anti-war resistance existed in the United States, in part because the newly acquired territory might be pro-slavery (or southern). Thus, internal sectional concerns also militated against the taking of even more land from Mexico. Such speculation aside, the border remains both a dividing line and a magnet that brings Mexican and U.S. citizens into close contact on a daily basis. Today's border, in other words, is an undeniable geographic fact of life that resulted from the war of 1846-1848. Yet that border cannot stop an irrepressible movement of goods, people, and ideas.

Three observations about the lasting geographic consequences of the war can be made. The first relates to the Southern Transcontinental Railroad, which was indeed constructed some thirty years *after* the War (1879-1881) as the Southern Pacific Railroad's "Sunset Route" was built from California to New Orleans by way of Yuma, Tucson, El Paso and San Antonio (the latter two cities along its Texas link, the Galveston, Harrisburg, and San Antonio Railroad). Farther north, predecessors of the Santa Fe Railroad built across New Mexico and Arizona by 1881 and 1882. Both of these major transcontinental railroads were completed in 1883. This railroad building soon reached well into Mexico as U.S. railroads would indeed connect with Pacific ports such as Guaymas and, later, Topolobampo. Railroad construction was frustrated, however, for nearly three decades by sectional conflict and economic crises in the United States, to name just two causes.

This fact has often led historians to downplay the role of railroads in the U.S.-Mexican War. But railroad fever did not *follow* the war, and was, in fact, prevalent well *before* the conflict. That railroad fever can be considered among the factors leading to U.S. expansionism is seen in the correspondence and literature of the time. A July 1845 letter in the *Niles National Register* in November of that year noted that "Albert M. Gilliam, late U.S. consul at California, is of the opinion that the government of California must soon fall into the hands of the American race, and that a railroad, direct from San Francisco, either to New Orleans or some point on the Red River, might be made to great advantage."[9] The year 1845 also witnessed agitation for railroads as evidenced by Asa Whitney's proposal to congress, and further noted at the conference on internal improvements at Memphis in October of that year.[10] Correspondence and newspapers of the period suggest that the railroads were viewed as an element in the arsenal of western expansionists—in some cases as early as the late 1820s; by the 1830s, Pacific Railroad promotion rhetoric reached a fever pitch. Regarding the causes of the U.S.-Mexican War, then, railroads were perceived as providing opportunities for U.S. expansion into what was then Mexico: it may therefore be said that the spectre of railroad development actually helped to precipitate the war, albeit indirectly.

The second geographic observation relates to mining: Despite various reconnaissance missions, Mexico had, with very few exceptions, done rather little to exploit or develop the mineral resources of its far northern frontier. Aside from small copper and silver mining operations in New Mexico and a small find of alluvial gold at Placeritas (California), mineral wealth seemed both remote and elusive in the

far north. It was this area that was subsequently developed aggres-
sively by Anglo-American mining interests in response to a growing
demand for metals as both specie and the raw materials of industry.
Those placer and hard-rock mining ventures by Anglo-Americans in
California, Arizona, Colorado, New Mexico and Nevada would reveal
the area that Mexico lost to be a virtual El Dorado of gold, copper,
and silver. History has shown that it was these mines that would be
developed using technology both originally developed by Mexican
mining interests and, through science and engineering, perfected by
the Anglo-Americans in the later nineteenth century. Ironically, the
discovery of placer gold in California very shortly *before* the end of the
struggle by James Marshall (a Mormon who had accompanied the
Mormon Battalion) soon revealed California to be a prize of unparal-
leled value. The Gold Rush that followed in 1849 brought in a flood
of Americans (and many peoples from around the world) and helped
further position the United States as a major economic force in world
affairs.

Lastly, one enduring geographic legacy of the U.S.-Mexican War to
the perceptual geography of both countries is somewhat invisible, but
appears in the many toponyms, or place names, that are a result of the
Spanish and Mexican colonization and settlement of today's American
Southwest. These include El Paso, Santa Fe and Albuquerque.
Moreover, place names peculiar to the war itself were adopted by communities in the United States to commemorate battles and campaigns—for example, Matamoros and Río Grande, Ohio; or Saltillo,
Pennsylvania. In Mexico, place names also commemorate numerous
important Mexican military figures associated with the war, so that the
geographic legacy of the conflict is never distant.

In many ways the conflict left geographical consequences and
repercussions that are still felt today. For historians on both sides of
the border, the geographic aspects of the war are vividly revealed in
both written records and in the rich cartographic legacy of map makers who endeavored to keep up with the rapid changes of those fate-
ful and tumultuous times. As illustrated in the many brochures and
publications of a century and a half ago, the landscape of the

Borderlands reflects the character of the two separate and unique countries that now share a common boundary with but a few minor modifications since 1854.

NOTES

1. David Weber, *The Spanish Frontier in North America* (New Haven: Yale University Press, 1992).

2. Charles M. Haecker, "Brazito Battlefield: Once Lost, Now Found." *New Mexico Historical Review*, Vol. 72 (July 1997), pp. 229-238.

3. Bryant Parrot Tilden. *Notes on the Upper Río Grande, [Explored in the months of October and November, 1846, on board the U.S. steamer Major Brown, commanded by Capt. Mark Sterling, of Pittsburgh. By order of Major General Patterson, USA commanding the Second Division, Army of Occupation, Mexico]* (Philadelphia: Lindsay & Blakiston, 1847).

4. Jack Jackson, "General Taylor's 'Astonishing' Map of Northeastern Mexico," *Southwestern Historical Quarterly*, Vol. 101 (October, 1997), pp. 142-173.

5. Angela Moyano Pahissa, *La Resistencia de las Californias a la Invasión Norteamericana (1846-1848)* (Mexico City: Consejo Nacional para la Cultura y las Artes, 1992); Doyce B. Nunis, Jr., ed., *The Mexican War in Baja California: The Memorandum of Captain Henry W. Halleck Concerning His Expedition in Lower California, 1846-1848* (Los Angeles: Dawson's Book Shop, 1977).

6. Paula Rebert, "Mapping the United States-Mexico Boundary: Cooperation and Controversy," *Terrae Incognitae—The Journal for the History of Discoveries*, Vol. 28 (1996), pp. 58-71.

7. See David Lavender, *The Southwest* (Albuquerque: University of New Mexico Press, 1984).

8. David Weber, "Turner, the Boltonians, and the Borderlands," *The American Historical Review*, Vol. 91 (February 1986), pp. 66-81.

9. *Niles National Register*, Vol. 19 (29 November 1845), p. 203.

10. See Norman A. Graebner, *Empire on the Pacific: A Study in American Continental Expansion* (Santa Barbara: ABC Clio, 1983)

2.
"But What Will England Say?"
Great Britain, the United States, and the War with Mexico

by Sam W. Haynes

In the months prior to the outbreak of hostilities with Mexico, few expansionists doubted that the United States would prevail in the event of war between the two countries. Jingoistic predictions of victory were often tempered, however, by the sobering realization that such a conflict might not be limited to a struggle between the two continental neighbors. One observer summed up both the national chauvinism and the concerns of expansionists in a letter to Caleb Cushing in August, 1845. "[I]f the sword is drawn the Saxons of the west must ultimately find sleep in the Mexican capital," C. Palmer of Richmond wrote to the renowned diplomat and politician. "But what will England say?"[1]

U.S. policy-makers in Washington shared Palmer's concern. Though ostensibly a neutral bystander, Her Majesty's government was viewed by the Polk administration as the root cause of many of the disputes that divided the United States and Mexico. As tensions between the two countries mounted over such issues as the legitimate boundary of Texas, the future status of California, and the Mexican government's refusal to receive John Slidell as U.S. minister, the president and his advisers often regarded Mexican leaders as little more than accomplices in a larger plot orchestrated by Great Britain to thwart U.S. interests. Such fears proved unfounded, and no sooner had the war begun than critics of the administration were quick to denounce the Democratic president for waging a war of conquest upon a weaker neighbor. This study examines the wider geopolitical context which dominated expansionist thinking in 1846, a context which prompted many to view the aggressive policy assumed by the United States against Mexico as a valid response to British ambitions.

Thirty years after the War of 1812, the historic enmity between Great Britain and its former colonies showed no signs of abating. Americans had long been suspicious of British activities in the western hemisphere, but inevitably this fear had grown as the United States defined its economic and strategic interests in terms that extended beyond its own borders. Of principal concern was the close relationship between Great Britain and Mexico. Great Britain had been quick to establish commercial treaties with many of the new Latin American republics in the 1820s, and two decades later remained Mexico's largest trading partner and principal source of capital investment. Though Anglo-Mexican relations were by no means always harmonious, Queen Victoria's diplomatic representatives enjoyed considerable influence in Mexico City. Unstable political conditions in Mexico only added to the concerns of U.S. expansionists, who viewed Mexican leaders as all the more dependent on their British allies.

During the early 1840s, Americans eager to annex the Republic of Texas accused the British of plotting to bring the fledgling nation back under Mexican rule. In fact, Her Majesty's government was publicly committed to a policy of preserving Texas' independence, but this did little to allay the suspicions of U.S. Anglophobes when, in 1842, Mexico ordered two warships from an English shipbuilding firm as part of its campaign to recover its former province. Although Her Majesty's government was in compliance with international neutrality laws, the two ships were not only built in England, but manned by English crews and commanded by officers on leaves of absence from the Royal Navy.[2] When Mexico invaded Texas in the spring of 1842, pro-annexation newspapers circulated as fact the rumor that the expedition had been financed with British capital. Complained the British consul in Texas to Foreign Secretary Lord Aberdeen: "The most strenuous endeavors have been made by the United States newspapers . . . to create and fix the impression that Mexico was secretly prompted by England in her persevering hostility to Texas."[3]

Allegations of British meddling in the affairs of Texas dominated expansionist propaganda in the drive toward annexation in 1844. But it was not until the spring of 1845, with Texas on the verge of admission into the Union, that substantive evidence came to light to support such charges. In early March, the U.S. Congress passed a joint resolution offering to annex the Lone Star Republic; all that now remained was for Texas to accept the agreement formally. But in a dramatic, eleventh hour bid to block a union between the two North American republics, Charles Elliot, Britain's chargé d'affaires to Texas, prevailed upon Texas President Anson Jones to delay action on the forthcoming U.S. annexation proposal for ninety days. Acting in concert with his French counterpart, Alphonse Dubois de Saligny, Elliot drafted a memorandum in which the government of Texas promised—pending approval by the voters of Texas—not to annex itself to the United States if Mexico would acknowledge the Republic's independence. Elliot traveled to Mexico City to obtain the Herrera government's acceptance of the memorandum, but unwisely decided to make the trip incognito. His identity was soon discovered, and by the time Elliot returned to Galveston in May his mission had become public knowledge in Texas and the United States.

Not surprisingly, the sensational news that Elliot had traveled in disguise on a secret mission to Mexico provoked a wave of anti-British feeling in the United States, corroborating long-standing suspicions of British activities toward Texas. In the Lone Star Republic, whatever public support for independence now vanished amid widespread fears that Texas would be little more than a client state of Great Britain. Vilified for his role in the affair and denounced as a tool of the British, Anson Jones called a convention for July 4 to decide the annexation question; the Republic's acceptance of the U.S. proposal now became a foregone conclusion.

Elliot's covert diplomacy had repercussions that extended well beyond the annexation of Texas. For nine years the Mexican government had refused to recognize the Republic's independence; its decision to abruptly reverse this policy was interpreted in Washington as proof positive that Mexican leaders took their instructions from Whitehall. Increasingly, the Polk administration would now view Mexican sovereignty as a fiction, its leaders eager to do the bidding of Her Majesty's government. Upon his return to Texas, Elliot managed only to heighten apprehensions that Great Britain was the guiding force behind Mexico. No doubt frustrated and aware that his efforts had been for naught, the British diplomat reportedly let it be known that if the American annexation proposal was accepted by the convention, Mexico would immediately declare war against the United States, sparking a conflagration that might well involve Great Britain.[4]

Elliot's actions and his none-too subtle threat of a British military alliance with Mexico shocked U.S. expansionists. "It is not for a moment to be supposed that Mexico would dream of war, if she were not urged to it by our foreign rivals," declared the New York Herald. Having followed the British diplomat's activities with keen interest, the U.S. chargé d'affaires to Texas, Andrew Jackson Donelson, wrote back to Washington to sound the alarm. Rather than view Elliot's recent mission to Mexico as the last-ditch effort of a failed diplomacy, Donelson viewed it in far more sinister terms, as "nothing more nor less than a contrivance of Great Britain" designed to inflame tensions between the neighboring countries. Her Majesty's government had engineered the Mexican peace overture with the knowledge that its rejection by the people of Texas would be interpreted as a hostile act by Mexican leaders, the U.S. chargé d'affaires informed Secretary of State James Buchanan on June 2. Having failed repeatedly in its attempts to thwart annexation by diplomatic means, Great Britain now intended to goad Mexico into "a war with the United States."[5] In an even more alarming dispatch two days later, Donelson offered further details of what he was now convinced was a British plot to initiate hostilities. So great was Donelson's fear of Elliot's influence that he had convinced himself that the British chargé d'affaires had the authority to launch a Mexican invasion of Texas. "Captain Elliott [sic], as soon as he is informed that he cannot defeat annexation, will be apt to find means of conveying secret intelligence to the commander of the Mexican troops on the Río Grande, who . . . will be prepared at once to resume the war upon Texas." The U.S. chargé d'affaires concluded his dispatch on a somber note: "I look upon war with Mexico as inevitable—a war dictated by the British minister here for the purpose of defeating annexation. . . ."[6]

Donelson's fears that the British were working actively behind the scenes to subvert annexation at any cost had no basis in fact. The U.S. chargé had greatly exaggerated the influence of his British counterpart, whose mission to Mexico had never been authorized by Her Majesty's government. Mindful of the wave of anti-British sentiment in Texas and the United States which Elliot's activities had caused, Lord Aberdeen censured his freewheeling diplomat and informed the U.S. minister to London that Elliot had acted on his own initiative.[7] Donelson's suspicions that the belligerent posture assumed by the Mexican government had been instigated by the British were equally unfounded. Far from encouraging Mexico to embark upon a war against its northern neighbor, Her Majesty's government had notified Mexican leaders that they could expect no aid from Great Britain should an invasion of Texas be attempted, a warning which they would repeat on numerous occasions in the months ahead.[8]

Nonetheless, Donelson's early June dispatches, with their dire warnings of British complicity in a Mexican campaign to reconquer Texas, created no small amount of excitement when they arrived in Washington. "In view of the facts disclosed by you, not only as regards the approach of an invading Mexican army, but of the open intermeddling of the Brittish [sic] Charge d'Affaires," the president wrote on June 15, "I have lost no time in causing the most prompt and energetic measures to be adopted here. I am resolved to defend and protect Texas as far as I possess the constitutional power to do so." Accordingly, the secretary of war sent an express messenger to Fort Jesup, Louisiana, ordering General Zachary Taylor to march his troops into Texas to repel an invasion. That same day, the president also ordered a naval buildup in the Gulf of Mexico. Once the convention accepted the annexation proposal on July 4, the United States would

be ready to "protect [Texans] against their Mexican enemies, stimu-
lated and excited as these enemies have been by Brittish [sic] intrigue
and influence."[9] Writing to Donelson in a similar vein, Secretary of
State Buchanan added "it would degrade the character of the United
States to suffer this great measure to be defeated…by the machinations of foreign Governments and the control they exercise over
Mexico."[10]

In a decision that would have enormous significance eleven
months later, the administration authorized Donelson to instruct
Taylor to take up positions *below* the Nueces River. Up to this point
Polk had been silent on the question of the boundary of Texas, which
he regarded as the principal stumbling block to the normalization of
relations between the United States and Mexico. While Texans since
the Revolution had claimed the Río Grande as the boundary of the
Republic, in 1845 many Anglo-Americans familiar with the territorial dispute had come to accept the need for compromise. Texas
President Anson Jones viewed the trans-Nueces as disputed territory, while the joint resolution of annexation so recently passed by the
U.S. Congress deliberately avoided any mention of the boundary
with Mexico, assuming the dispute could be resolved at a later date.
While Polk himself had not taken a clear stand on this question, his
campaign literature during the 1844 election insisted that the
boundary dispute should not be allowed to disrupt relations between
the United States and Mexico. Dismissing the Whig charge that
annexation would lead inevitably to war, the Democrats insisted that
Mexico would be compensated for the trans-Nueces region claimed
by Texas, and would, therefore, have no just cause of complaint. "Let
us pay her liberally for any just claim she may have against that country," declared a broadsheet issued by Democrats in Polk's home state
of Tennessee.[11]

But during the early summer of 1845, Polk was less interested in
sorting out which nation had the more valid claim to the region
than in presenting the United States as the protector of Texas.
Reacting to the perceived threat of a British-sponsored Mexican
invasion with a belligerence that worried even expansionist mem-

bers of his own party, Washington aimed to send a clear and unequivocal message to Mexico and Great Britain that it would brook no interference in its plans to annex Texas; it further wished to demonstrate to wavering Texans unhappy with the terms of the U.S. annexation offer that it could rely upon the United States to defend their interests. In so doing, the administration not only committed itself to the military protection of Texas, but to something far more controversial: the defense of a boundary claim that to many Americans seemed extravagant and unwarranted, and which the Mexican government regarded as grounds for war.

On the other side of the Atlantic, Her Majesty's government tried to allay American fears that Great Britain was intent on manufacturing a war between Mexico and the United States. Edward Everett, the U.S. minister to London, and his successor, Louis McLane, relayed these assurances to Washington, but their reports seem to have had little effect on U.S. policy-makers.[12] Having refused to accept Lord Aberdeen's public disavowals of undue interference in the affairs of Texas in 1844, and been so alarmed by Elliot's meddling in the annexation question in the early summer of 1845, the Anglophobic president and his advisers were disinclined to take British diplomats at their word.

Indeed, with the annexation of Texas now secure, Washington's fear of British machinations did not subside, but rather manifested itself in another part of the hemisphere. Britain's interest in adding the harbors of California to its global commercial empire had long been a source of concern to American expansionists. Since the early 1840s the U.S. press had periodically caught wind of rumors that Mexico might cede California to Great Britain in exchange for the assumption of Mexico's debt obligations to British creditors. In the fall of 1842, Commodore Thomas Ap Catesby Jones briefly seized Monterey, California, acting on the erroneous belief that Mexico, backed by Great Britain, had declared war against the United States.

Even prominent Whigs, mindful of the enormous commercial potential of California harbors, could sound Anglophobic when discussing Mexico's northernmost province. "Mexico, single handed, could not affect us much by any belligerent operations," observed Henry Clay, Polk's opponent in the recent election. "But Mexico, acting as an ally of Great Britain, is capable of inflicting upon us much mischief, especially on the Pacific...."[13] Declared Waddy Thompson, the former U.S. minister to Mexico during the Tyler administration: "It will be worth a war of twenty years to prevent England acquiring it."[14] In a rare spirit of bipartisanship, the Whig journal *American Review* urged the Polk administration to secure California before the prize fell to Great Britain, a nation motivated not only by "her general lust of colonial possessions," but the desire to create "a barrier to the growth in wealth, dominion and power of the American Union," which would serve to check "the progress of republican liberty, by which she believes her own institutions...to be seriously menaced."[15]

During the summer and fall of 1845, in the wake of Elliot's mission to Mexico, the expansionist press fueled American suspicions of British activities on the Pacific Coast. Great Britain had been foiled in its efforts to turn Texas into a British satellite; it would now devote its full attention to gaining control of California as part of its long term strategy to encircle the United States. The *New York Herald* went so far as to suggest that British interest in the Oregon territory was merely a ruse, asserting that "the real object of English cupidity is the acquisition of California."[16] Particularly alarming to the administration was the letter it received on October 11 from Thomas O. Larkin, the U.S. consul in Monterey and a devoted propagandist for U.S. expansion in California. Larkin claimed, among other things, that the British were financing a military expedition to suppress a new separatist government in California to bring the region back under Mexican control.[17] Information from other U.S. agents in the days that followed seemed to lend credence to such reports.[18] As in Texas, the administration saw the hand of the British working actively to thwart its territorial objectives. And, again as in Texas, Americans saw Great Britain attempting to use Mexico as a military surrogate to achieve its ends.

Suddenly apprehensive, Washington now began to regard California as a matter requiring its immediate attention. Accordingly,

James Buchanan

An engraving of James Buchanan. New York: Johnson, Fry, & Co., 1864. (Mexican War Graphics Collection, Special Collections Division, The University of Texas at Arlington Libraries, Arlington, Texas.)

the administration dispatched Marine Lieutenant Archibald Gillespie with orders for Larkin and John D. Sloat, commander of the Pacific Squadron. Larkin was instructed to ascertain whether Great Britain or France aimed to take control of the territory, and to warn the inhabitants of California of the dangers of European interference. Sloat, who had already been instructed to seize San Francisco and other strategic points in the event of hostilities, was advised to remain on alert. Commodore Robert F. Stockton, commander of the frigate *Congress*, was ordered to proceed immediately to the west coast.[19]

This new sense of urgency also prompted the administration to instruct its newly appointed minister to Mexico, John Slidell, to put Mexican leaders on notice that the United States would take steps to prevent the cession of California to any European power. Echoing his earlier instructions to Andrew Jackson Donelson, Secretary of State James Buchanan emphasized to Slidell that one of the "principal objects" of his mission would be "[t]o counteract the influence of foreign Powers, exerted against the United States in Mexico...."[20] Although Buchanan urged Slidell to be vigilant against the efforts of France, Buchanan left no doubt that "the cession of California to Great Britain, our principal commercial rival...would be most disastrous."[21]

Slidell's diplomatic errand caused a firestorm of protest in Mexico, which regarded the proposal to buy California and New Mexico as nothing less than an invitation to participate in the dismemberment of the national domain. No sooner had Slidell disembarked at Veracruz than Washington's offer to purchase New Mexico and California became public knowledge. Opposition newspapers were quick to accuse the Herrera regime of selling out to the United States. The headline of one newspaper screamed "The Treason has been discovered!"[22]

In fact, Slidell's instructions would be out of date within days of his arrival. While the president was well aware of the enormous commercial advantages to be gained by the acquisition of ports on the Pacific, Polk's eagerness to force the issue waxed and waned in direct proportion to his suspicions of British activities in the region. Thus when another dispatch from U.S. Consul Larkin arrived in December, seeming to indicate that the area was in no immediate danger from the British, the president modified his instructions to Slidell. If Mexican leaders showed no interest in selling California, the U.S. envoy was told, he should not allow the issue to upset the chances for normalizing relations between the two countries.[23]

But the damage to Herrera had already been done. Discredited for its apparent truckling to the United States, the government was overthrown in mid-December by the military leader Mariano Paredes. Slidell initially did not lament the passing of the Herrera regime, taking the view that a new government might be in a stronger position to negotiate with the United States. The U.S. diplomat's hopes for the success of his mission soon proved groundless. Adopting a strong anti-U.S. posture, Paredes showed little interest in reaching an accord, which Slidell and other Americans on the scene in Mexico City were quick to attribute to the influence of Great Britain. In late December Slidell reported to Washington that Charles Bankhead, the British minister to Mexico, had advised the new Mexican government to reject Slidell's credentials as U.S. minister, a charge the British diplomat denied. More circumspect than Donelson, Slidell did not believe that Her Majesty's government wished to provoke a war between the United States and Mexico. Nonetheless the U.S. diplomat remained convinced that Bankhead, acting on orders from Whitehall, would do all he could to disrupt the normalization of diplomatic relations between the two countries.[24]

During the early months of 1846, Washington's anxiety regarding European interference in the affairs of its Latin American neighbor increased with the news that Paredes was considering a plan to return Mexico to Spanish monarchical rule. Once again, on the basis of Slidell's dispatches from Mexico, the administration came to believe that the scheme had the covert sanction of Great Britain, which would receive Cuba for its part in the plan.[25] Reacting to rumors of the monarchist plot with the same anxiety with which he had responded to earlier reports of European designs in California, Secretary of State Buchanan instructed Slidell: "Should Great Britain and France attempt to place a Spanish or any other European Prince upon the throne of Mexico, this would be resisted by all the power of the United States. In opposition to such an attempt, party distinctions in this country would vanish and the people would be nearly unanimous."[26] Paredes' plan had little broad-based support in Mexico, however, and merely added to the confusion of an already chaotic political scene.

Despite deteriorating relations with Mexico, both U.S. policymakers and the general public remained preoccupied with another foreign policy crisis that involved a far more overt threat of war with Great Britain. In August, 1845, Polk had broken off negotiations with the British over the Oregon territory, and seemed intent on forcing a showdown with Her Majesty's government over the issue. In a move that was widely regarded as an ominous first step toward hostilities, Polk in his first annual message in December, 1845, called upon Congress to end the joint occupation of Oregon and assume full control of the territory, British claims to the region notwithstanding. In Polk's mind, the danger of hostilities with Mexico had clearly passed. Sidestepping the Mexican claim to the trans-Nueces, Polk stated blandly that American dominion had been "peacefully extended to the [Rio Grande] del Norte." The *Niles' National Register* summed up the nation's priorities in February, 1846, when it said: "Oregon throws Mexican affairs completely in the shade, for the time being."[27]

While the president insisted that the two crises were unrelated, both he and his advisers harbored little doubt that Mexico and Great Britain, acting either independently or in concert, would try to exploit the situation, assuming that the United States would not dare to fight a war with both nations. Thus the unwillingness of the Paredes government to reach a settlement with Washington, the administration concluded, stemmed from Mexico's belief that U.S.-British relations would continue to deteriorate. Still waiting for the Paredes government to receive him in the early months of 1846, Slidell was convinced that the success of his mission hinged upon the resolution of the Oregon crisis. No accommodation on the part of the Mexican government could be expected, Slidell believed, unless the Polk administration resumed negotiations with Her Majesty's government over the settlement of the boundary dispute in the Pacific northwest.[28]

To be sure, Mexico continued to hope that Great Britain would interpose to prevent further territorial acquisitions by the United States in the western hemisphere. Almost from the day Paredes assumed power in December, 1845, he enjoined, then pleaded with the British government to side with Mexico in its imminent conflict with the United States.[29] But in the final analysis, the Paredes regime's defiance in the face of ever-increasing diplomatic and military pressure from the Polk administration stemmed not from geopolitical considerations, but from a determination to salvage what remained of the nation's honor. Like Donelson in Texas and Larkin in California, Slidell failed to understand that Mexican leaders were capable of acting unilaterally and without regard for the long-range interests of their British allies. Thus despite British entreaties to resolve the crisis, the Paredes government refused to negotiate with the U.S. diplomatic representative, who in mid-March demanded his passports and sailed for home. With Slidell's departure, all hope for a negotiated settlement between the United States and Mexico came to an end. Five weeks later, Mexican troops crossed the Río Grande and engaged a small detachment of Taylor's force, thus precipitating the war between the two countries.

When Polk delivered his war message to Congress on May 11, the Oregon crisis remained unresolved, prompting many Americans to fear that the fighting in the trans-Nueces would erupt into a wider war between Great Britain and the United States. Anxious to deny Great Britain any pretext to side with Mexico, Secretary of State James Buchanan drew up a statement of the war's causes, which he intended to send to U.S. ministers overseas, explicitly disavowing any interest in acquiring more territory from Mexico. Polk, who had for several months hoped to acquire California, either by peaceful cession or as an indemnity in the event of hostilities, insisted that Buchanan delete any reference to the "no territory" pledge. When the secretary remarked that "he thought it almost certain that both England and France would join with Mexico in the war against us," the President replied: "I told him that the war with Mexico was an affair with which neither England, France, or any other power had any concern.... I told him there was no connection between the Oregon & Mexican question[s]," and that rather than give such a pledge "I would let the war which he apprehended with England come and would take the whole responsibility."[30]

Buchanan's concern that hostilities with Mexico might involve the United States in a war with a far more powerful adversary was shared by many Americans. The prospect of a war with Great Britain was the subject of much discussion among the soldiers stationed along the Río Grande. "I really think that four months will settle the affair with Mexico, unless England sides with her, in which event we shall have a war such as the world has not seen for many years," wrote George Gordon Meade, an officer in Taylor's army, in late May.[31] As the nation mobilized for war, even popular songs combined the strident jingoism of the day with a concern that Great Britain might well take a role in the contest. Compositions such as *A Song for the Army* left little doubt that while U.S. soldiers were marching off to fight Mexico, the real threat to American security interests lay elsewhere:

> And should old England interfere,
> to stop us in our bright career,
> We'll teach her, as we did of yore,
> This land is ours from shore to shore...
>
> So don't molest us, Johnny Bull,
> Or you may get your belly full;
> Hard words with you we would not bandy,
> For hard fighting has become quite handy...
>
> Let recreant statesmen fly the course,
> And General Scott, the old war-horse,
>
> Blow hot or cold his "plate of soup,"
> To England we will never stoop.[32]

Once war had been declared, the president moved promptly to seize strategic points along the Pacific coastline. With its fleet already patrolling the waters of the Pacific Coast, Washington now instructed Sloat to seize San Francisco. Despite Polk's remark to Buchanan that he would face a war with Great Britain with equanimity, the threat of British intervention remained a significant factor in the administration's war strategy, since Her Majesty's government had stated in December that it would "view with much dissatisfaction" any attempt by a foreign power to establish hegemony over California.[33] By establishing U.S. control over the region, the president intended to present Her Majesty's government with a *fait accompli* which, he hoped, would discourage the British from further action. Polk's instincts proved correct; although certain members of Her Majesty's government argued vigorously in favor of a military response to the U.S. seizure of California, both Peel and Foreign Secretary Lord Aberdeen were reluctant to risk a war with the United States with a resolution to the Oregon question now in sight.[34]

In fact, American military leaders in the West were already taking steps to secure Washington's territorial objectives even before the war began. At the center of these extraordinary events was the renowned explorer John Charles Frémont, now on his third expedition of the West. Prior to setting out on his mission in June, 1845, Frémont and his father-in-law, Missouri Senator Thomas Hart Benton, had discussed at length the dangers of allowing California to fall into British hands. Although Benton had no authority to speak for the administration, Frémont would later claim to have been given confidential knowledge of the "wishes, and...intentions" of the government with regard to California in the event of war between the United States, Mexico and Great Britain.[35] The first week in May, 1846, found Frémont near the California-Oregon border, where he met up with Polk's envoy, Archibald Gillespie. The marine lieutenant communicated to Frémont the contents of the administration's dispatch to Larkin, and turned over a packet of letters from Senator Benton and other family members. On the basis of this information, Frémont concluded that a British invasion was imminent, and that he should "not let the English get possession of California, but should use any means in his power, or any occasion that offered, to prevent such a thing."[36] In his memoirs written many years later, Frémont recalled: "The time has come. England must not get a foothold. We must be first."[37]

In Mexico City, meanwhile, American diplomats remained convinced that Mexican leaders were acting at the behest of their British allies. Four weeks after U.S. and Mexican troops clashed in the trans-Nueces, U.S. Consul John Black, Washington's principal contact in Mexico City after Slidell's departure, continued to emphasize the close relationship between Paredes and Her Majesty's government. "[A]lthough [Great Britain] has not visibly committed herself in this affair," Black reported, "yet she is the Secret Spring that has set all this Machinery in Motion, and that she will not fail to make every effort in her power to bring about her darling object by means of a wily diplomacy." According to Black, Her Majesty's government aimed to mediate in the dispute, in exchange for which she would receive from Mexico territory "to hem in the United States," commercial privileges, and loan guarantees. "She has not only the present administration on her side, but also the leading dignitaries of the Church, and her gold can secure the army."[38] William S. Parrott, a confidential agent sent to Mexico, agreed, stating flatly that "Mexico may be said to be completely in the hands of England."[39]

As usual, this disturbing intelligence contrasted sharply with the views of the U.S. minister to London, Louis McLane. Not only did McLane dismiss the likelihood of British involvement in hostilities between the United States and Mexico, he doubted that Mexican leaders would even be able to secure a loan from British banking houses with which to prosecute a war. In several meetings with the U.S. minister, Foreign Secretary Lord Aberdeen repeatedly denied "in the most explicit terms," that Great Britain was seeking to exacerbate tensions between the United States and Mexico.[40] On the contrary, in a meeting in mid-June, Aberdeen read to McLane the contents of a dispatch to Charles Bankhead, the British minister to Mexico, disclaiming any interest in siding with Mexico, and urging that government to reach an amicable agreement with the United States.[41]

Although McLane was troubled by the hostility toward the United States in the British press, he doubted that it would have any effect on Her Majesty's government, and by August he could confidently state that as long as the U.S. blockade of Mexican ports did not violate British neutrality rights, "there will be no attempt on the part of [Her Majesty's] government to interfere."[42]

In the weeks that followed Polk's declaration of war, it became evident that Great Britain intended to take no role in the conflict with Mexico. Far more interested in the simmering conflict over Oregon, Her Majesty's government responded quickly to the joint resolution passed by Congress calling for an "amicable settlement" of the dispute, proposing a compromise similar to the one which its minister to Washington, Richard Pakenham, had rejected the previous year. By the summer of 1846, any lingering fears that Great Britain would never permit the United States to establish a continental empire—a long-standing shibboleth of U.S. Anglophobes—had been effectively laid to rest by the Senate's ratification of the Oregon treaty and the U.S. seizure of California. To be sure, U.S. citizens remained suspicious of British intentions; when Lord Aberdeen suggested British mediation to resolve the conflict with Mexico, the offer was politely but firmly rejected by the Polk administration. Many expansionists, like James Gordon Bennett of the *New York Herald*, worried that England might "furnish the means to Mexico to carry on and protract the war, with the hope of making Mexico still further dependent upon her than she is," a concern that grew when a string of American victories failed to bring the negotiated settlement U.S. policy-makers had anticipated.[43] But the specter of direct British military involvement, which had played such a conspicuous part in the shaping American policies in Texas, Oregon and California, quickly faded as the nation devoted its energies to the conquest of Mexico.

All this is not to suggest that a war with Mexico could have been avoided without the threat of Great Britain; by the mid-1840s the United States had acquired a voracious appetite for new territories that could only be satisfied at Mexico's expense. Nonetheless the Polk administration's determined, belligerent policies were at least in part a response to the belief that Great Britain would seek to take maximum advantage of the neighbors of the United States to thwart Polk's territorial ambitions. Just as evidence of British meddling in Texas had stiffened the resolve of U.S. expansionists to bring the Republic into the Union, the close alliance of Great Britain and Mexico created a sense of anxiety in Washington that precluded calm, non-aggressive diplomatic initiatives.

To some historians, the conflict that ensued between the United States and Mexico has invited comparison with the Vietnam War.[44] The U.S.-Mexican War, like the conflict in which this country would become embroiled more than a century later, was denounced as a war of aggression by administration critics, who would become more vocal and more numerous as the war dragged on. "But Mr. Polk's War" may be analogous to the conflict in Southeast Asia in still another way, for in both cases the United States declared war upon a weaker nation which it viewed as a surrogate of a world power that seemed—at least to U.S. policy-makers—to represent a serious threat to national security interests. Just as U.S. foreign policy misadventures in the underdeveloped world after World War II must be viewed in the larger context of Cold War tensions, the vigorous expansionism of Manifest Destiny was shaped in large part by the nation's adversarial relationship with Great Britain. In the calculus on tensions leading up to the U.S.-Mexican War, what England might say—and, more importantly, what England might do—was never far from the minds of Polk and his advisors.

NOTES

1. C. Palmer to Caleb Cushing, August 14, 1845, quoted in John Belohlavek, "Race, Progress and Destiny: Caleb Cushing and the Quest for American Empire," Sam W. Haynes and Christopher Morris, eds., *Manifest Destiny and Empire: American Antebellum Expansionism* (College Station: Texas A & M University Press, 1997) p. 39.

2. Ephraim D. Adams, *British Activities in Texas, 1838-1846* (Gloucester, Massachusetts: Peter Smith, 1963), ch. 4, passim.

3. Joseph Milton Nance, *Attack and Counter-Attack: The Texas-Mexican Frontier, 1842* (Austin: University of Texas Press, 1964), p. 138; Kennedy to Aberdeen, June 15, 1842, Ephraim D. Adams, ed., *British Diplomatic Correspondence Concerning the Republic of Texas, 1836-1846* (Austin: Texas State Historical Association, 1917), p. 69.

4. Justin Smith, *Annexation of Texas* (New York: AMS Press, 1971, reprint) p. 449.

5. Donelson to Buchanan, June 2, 1845, Senate Documents, 29th Congress, 1st session, No. 26, pp. 64-66; New York *Herald*, September 2, 1845.

6. Donelson to Buchanan, June 4, 1845, Senate Documents, 29th Congress, 1st session, No. 27, pp. 66-67.

7. Aberdeen to Elliot, July 3, 1845, Ephraim D. Adams, ed., *British Diplomatic Correspondence*, pp. 508, 510; Edward Everett to James Buchanan, July 4, 1845, William Manning, ed., *Diplomatic Correspondence of the United States, Inter-American Affairs* (hereafter cited as *DCUS-IAA*) vol. 7, p. 270. (Washington, D.C: Carnegie Endowment for International Peace, 1932-1939).

8. Sam W. Haynes, *Soldiers of Misfortune: The Somervell and Mier Expeditions* (Austin: University of Texas Press, 1990), pp.197-98.

9. James K. Polk to Donelson, June 15, 1845, "Letters of James K. Polk to Andrew J. Donelson, 1843-1848," *Tennessee Historical Magazine*, vol. 3 (Mar.-Dec. 1917), pp. 67-68.

10. Buchanan to Donelson, June 15, 1845, John Bassett Moore, ed., *The Works of James Buchanan* (New York: Antiquarian Press, 1960), vol. 6, p. 172.

11. *Annexation of Texas to the United States* (Nashville: John P. Heiss, 1844), p. 14.

12. Edward Everett to James Buchanan, July 4, 1845, *DCUS-IAA*, vol. 7, p. 270; Louis McLane to James Buchanan, September 26, 1845, Ibid., vol. 7, pp. 270-71.

13. Henry Clay to John Lawrence, April 30, 1845, James F. Hopkins et. al., eds., *The Papers of Henry Clay* (Lexington: University of Kentucky Press, 1959), vol. 10, pp. 223-24.

14. Waddy Thompson, *Recollections of Mexico* (New York: Wiley and Putnam, 1846), p. 235.

15. "California," *American Review*, vol. 3 (January, 1846), p. 98.

16. New York *Herald*, July 30, 1845.

17. Thomas O. Larkin to James Buchanan, July 10, 1845, Manning, ed., *DCUS-IAA*, vol. 8, p. 736.

18. David Pletcher, *The Diplomacy of Annexation: Texas, Oregon and the Mexican War* (Columbia: University of Missouri Press, 1973), pp. 281-82.

19. Ibid., pp. 283-84.

20. James Buchanan to John Slidell, November 10, 1845, Manning, ed., *DCUS-IAA*, vol. 8 p. 172.

21. Ibid., vol. 8, p. 180.

22. Dennis E. Berge, "Mexican Response to United States' Expansionism, 1841-1848," Ph.D. Dissertation, University of California at Berkeley, 1965, p. 175.

23. Thomas O. Larkin to James Buchanan, September 29, 1845, Manning, ed., *DCUS-IAA*, vol. 8, p. 755; James Buchanan to John Slidell, December 17, 1845, Ibid., vol. 8, p. 184.

24. John Slidell to James Buchanan, December 29, 1845, Ibid., vol. 8, p. 805.

25. New Orleans *Daily Picayune*, December 30, 1845.

26. James Buchanan to John Slidell, March 12, 1846, Manning, ed., *DCUS-IAA*, vol. 8, p. 192.

27. *Niles' National Register*, February 21, 1846.

28. James Buchanan to John Slidell, February 6, 1845, Manning, ed., *DCUS-IAA*, vol. 8, p. 811.

29. Pletcher, *Diplomacy of Annexation*, p. 370; John Paul Tymitz, "British Influence in Mexico, 1840-1848," Ph.D. Dissertation, Oklahoma State University, 1973, p. 147.

30. Justin Smith, *The War with Mexico* (New York: Macmillan, 1919), vol. 1, pp. 397-98.

31. George Meade, *The Life and Letters of General George Gordon Meade* (New York: Charles Scribner's Sons, 1913), vol. 1, p. 96.

32. William McCarty, comp., *National Songs, Ballads, and Other Patriotic Poetry, Chiefly Relating to the War of 1846* (Philadelphia: W. McCarty, 1846), pp. 77-78.

33. Adams, *British Interests and Activities in Texas*, p. 248.

34. Pletcher, *Diplomacy of Annexation*, p. 424.

35. John Charles Fremont, *Memoirs of My Life* (Chicago: Belford, Clarke & Co., 1887), vol. 1, p. 423.

36. Allan Nevins, *Fremont: Pathmarker of the West* (New York: Ungar, 1961), p. 244.

37. Fremont, *Memoirs of My Life*, vol. 1, p. 489.

38. John Black to James Buchanan, May 23, 1846, Manning, ed., *DCUS-IAA*, vol. 8, p. 854.

39. Smith, *The War with Mexico*, vol. 1, p. 443n.

40. Louis McLane to James Buchanan, September 26, 1845, Manning, ed., *DCUS-IAA*, vol. 7, p. 271; Same to same, May 18, 1846, Ibid., vol. 7, p. 274.

41. McLane to Buchanan, June 18, 1846, Ibid., vol. 7, p. 283.

42. McLane to Buchanan, August 15, 1846, Ibid., vol. 7, pp. 286-87.

43. New York *Herald*, May 21, 1846.

44. This argument is made forcefully by John H. Schroeder, *Mr. Polk's War: American Opposition and Dissent, 1846-1848* (Madison: University of Wisconsin Press, 1973).

3.
Causes of the War with the United States

by Josefina Zoraida Vázquez
as translated by Douglas W. Richmond

One hundred and fifty years later, Mexicans remain profoundly angered by the war between Mexico and the United States. In the North American historical conscience, the war has always been ignored, apparently "overshadowed by the cataclysmic Civil War."[1] But its historians have lost, in large part, the cynical attitude of Justin Smith or Samuel Bemis and fine books such as David Pletcher, *The Diplomacy of Annexation: Texas, Oregon and the Mexican War*,[2] Robert W. Johannsen, *To the Halls of the Montezumas: The Mexican War in the American Imagination*,[3] and John S. D. Eisenhower, *So Far From God: The U.S. War With Mexico, 1846-1848* have appeared. The internal Mexican situation at the time of the war, which North Americans as well as many Mexican scholars had not described well, has now been clarified. Two books that give the first national accounts of the political effects and regional reactions of the different states to the war are Pedro Santoni, *Mexicans at Arms: Puro Federalists and the Politics of War, 1845-1848* and Josefina Zoraida Vázquez, ed., *México al tiempo de su guerra con Estados Unidos, 1846-1848*.[4] Nevertheless, a task that remains is ending the unjust accusation that attributes to Mexico much of the blame for starting the war. For Mexico, the war left an uncomfortable feeling of not being able to deal better with its defense.

North American historiography has elucidated all aspects of the war: battles, strategy, weapons, casualties, desertions, background of the soldiers, finances and regional variations. Mexican scholars, until recently, have preferred to avoid the war, as well as the thankless period of national life that proceeds from independence to the end of the conflict. Discussion on two themes continue: the causes of the war and the Mexican political scene.

Today it is generally accepted that the principal cause of the war was North American expansionism, although interpretations vary over the sparks that finally detonated the opening salvos of the conflict.

Superficial accounts of the war still mention contemporary justifications of the event: the North American "necessity" to avoid Great Britain taking over California, the "warlike" Mexicans, and the slowness of the Mexican government in refusing to sell a territory that it was inevitably going to lose. Nevertheless, the most unknown and worst represented aspect is Mexico's complex internal situation; historian David Pletcher has summarized it in an insensitive caricature:

> Mexico was a sick country, with the national equivalent of dropsy, intermittent fever, a creeping paralysis. In the cruel world of nineteenth-century Machpolitek, her illness inspired in her ambitious neighbor more cupidity than sympathy.[5]

This paragraph is unworthy of a profession whose goal is to comprehend and omit the territorial ambitions that began much earlier when New Spain (or colonial Mexico) was prosperous and had still not been affected by the disunity, bankruptcy, and unfortunate wars that it would inherit from its European metropolis, followed by a bloody struggle for independence and foreign threats. From classic studies such as Frederick Merk's *Manifest Destiny and Mission in American History*, we know that the early expression of expansionism affected all regions of the United States and that all its areas embraced it up to the convenient limits of "the color line of the Río Grande."[6]

Mexican historians have always viewed expansionism as the origin of the war, with the independence and annexation of Texas as the immediate cause and the North American infiltration into California as an aggravating provocation. For this reason, during the war

Mexicans referred to it as "the Texas War." It was not until the landing of Winfield Scott in Veracruz that it became known as "the North American intervention." Since the publication of *Apuntes para la guerra entre México y los Estados Unidos* (1848), Mexicans do not consider the origins of the war covered in mystery and they affirm that "it is enough to say that the war was caused by the insatiable ambition of the United States, aided by our weakness."[7]

Today our historical knowledge permits us to see the phenomenom in the broad context of universal history, whose events favored the appearance of the United States and Brazil, but not their other southern neighbors.

The independence of the thirteen colonies and of the kingdom of New Spain and the rest of Hispanic America resulted in large measure from the Seven Years War and the bankruptcies produced in the participating countries. To resolve this, Great Britain and Spain reorganized their governments and established new fiscal demands upon their colonies, which fomented great discontent among the inhabitants. But New Spain, the most important kingdom of the Spanish empire, was at its greatest prosperity and with tight bonds to the metropolis, which retarded its breaking away.

The antecedents of the two republics influenced their development as independent countries. The thirteen colonies were established in the seventeenth century—a period of modernity—while Mexico resulted from conquest at the beginning of the sixteenth century—an era still with medieval traits. This did not impede New Spain from becoming a wealthy, prosperous and distinguished kingdom, such that the eighteenth century in New Spain contrasts itself to the provincialism of the thirteen colonies.

The American colonies not only appeared at the time of the Puritan revolution, but before the organization of the British empire, when the more valuable and successful West Indies flourished, which allowed the thirteen colonies to acquire a certain amount of governmental experience. Moreover, the appearance of the United States as an independent nation was favored by diverse circumstances that hastened the difficulties of its Mexican neighbor. In the context of the enlightened era, before the excesses of the French revolution, the Anglo-American struggle for independence in defense of liberties and the right to representation against tyranny aroused sympathies. This encouraged the possibility of Spanish and French retaliation against Great Britain for the defeat that London had inflicted on them, thus converting Spain and France into allies. The Anglo-American elite could mobilize a society not constrained by the widespread violence that characterized newly liberated Hispanic America—although American society was corrupted by slavery. The independence struggle was brief, favored by political division within British diplomatic isolation so that little bloodshed resulted. Therefore, before consummating independence, the new nation had been recognized by France (1778) and Holland (1780) and, by 1783, its own metropolis with a peace treaty that permitted the United States to enter the international arena with full rights.

The United States could also count upon other blessings: the same year that it consolidated its political organization (1789), the French revolution broke out, which initiated a quarter of a century of European warfare. The new nation took advantage and was able to expand its commerce under the flag of neutrality, absorb immigrants, and experiment with a political system that assured the constant growth of its population and economy without European interference.

New Spain would not have the same luck. The modernization of the Spanish empire, the professionalization of its administrative apparatus and the developing structures in the colony divided its elite on the eve of the profound crisis that confronted the empire when it lost its king in 1808. The Spanish reforms increased financial revenues, but the metropolitan government extracted vast sums from Mexico to support its ongoing European wars. By 1800, New Spain was bankrupt even before beginning its struggle for independence and had started to be the target of the commercial powers. Mexican silver was indispensable for war, business, and basic needs—just as much for Great Britain and France as well as Spain.

A New Spain that was indebted, decapitalized, with a fragmented elite, a population impoverished by tax increases and a prolonged drought, now suffered a long and bloody independence struggle in which she could not count on allies, not even the United States, among those who waited for Mexico's colonial status to end. After eleven years, Mexico entered independence bloodied and with a ruined economy. Bankruptcy and political inexperience were shaky foundations on which to construct a new state over an immense territory without effective communications and a heterogeneous, badly distributed population.

The international context was not propitious. Europe was peaceful yet fearful of the liberalism that permeated the independence movements and determined to defend the traditional rights of the monarchies. The resulting legitimacy of the liberal tone made it difficult for Europe to recognize the new states. Mexico's metropolis, without resigning itself to losing its ex-colony, not only refused to recognize it—which was Spanish policy until 1836—but, fortified by the Holy Alliance, threatened Mexico with reconquest. The British, so interested in Mexican silver and its market, were very late in breaking their commitments to Spain.

In this manner, up to 1821, while the economy and population of the United States doubled thanks to four decades of stable government dominated by an impressive elite, Mexico lost its old dynamism. The social division was profound, the population had been reduced by the loss of 600,000 lives—half the labor force—and the independence struggle had fragmented the administrative and economic networks.

The new nation inherited the Hispanic greatness and prosperity of the eighteenth century, but also a certain vulnerability that awakened European and North American ambitions to the point that Mexico became converted into the most threatened nation on the continent during most of the nineteenth century. All this combined to block Mexico's recuperation and the consolidation of a stable government.

Therefore, while in 1804 the two countries had similar populations and territory, by 1821 a certain asymmetry was already apparent; by the 1840s it was even greater—the northern country had a population of almost twenty million while Mexico counted a few more than seven million inhabitants.

A detail from the *Mapa de los Estados Unidos de Mejico*. Philadelphia: J. Disturnell, 1846.
(Cartographic History Library, Special Collections Division, The University of Texas at
Arlington Libraries, Arlington, Texas.)

For Mexico, which started its independence in 1821, the success of the North American political system converted the United States into a model to imitate; but the threat from the north would not go away. With the northern example in mind, the republican option defeated the monarchist sentiment in a rather brusque manner. Taking into consideration the northern model, Mexico hoped that colonization would be the best way to encourage prosperity in its northern frontier. For these reasons, Mexico conceded more favorable conditions to settlers than did the North American government. Therefore, the loss of Texas was very painful to Mexico.

It was natural that the Texas question would affect relations between Mexico and the United States. Although the Texas revolt was a Mexican internal problem, President Andrew Jackson declared U.S. neutrality. Nevertheless, he did not uphold this stance; Jackson permitted the free entrance of an avalanche of North American volunteers and arms to Texas accompanied by a mobilization of troops under the command of General E.P. Gaines to the Sabine River boundary to avoid the possibility that Indians, Texans, and Mexicans would "violate North American territory." Gaines was also authorized to advance up to Nacogdoches. Lacking any reply to his protests, Manuel Eduardo de Gorostiza, the Mexican minister in Washington, requested his passports and returned to Mexico.[8]

The Texas revolt eliminated from the North American agenda the purchase of the province, which had monopolized U.S. diplomatic instructions sent to Mexico. Minister Powathan Ellis' instructions, which arrived in April, 1836, centered on pressuring the Mexican government to pay reparations.[9] President Jackson's true strategy attempted to weaken the Mexican position at the moment when Mexico undertook the expedition to subdue the Texas rebellion.

The reparations were a tangle of cases that affected diverse groups, authorities, localities and nationalities. The North Americans claimed damages and debts from the independence struggle. The majority of the claims were unacceptable or exaggerated, however.[10] Many covered commercial and fiscal areas: forced loans, double payment of taxes, property damages during disturbances. Only a small part referred to the exercise of justice: accusations of concubinage, assassination, participating in invasions or introducing items not expressly prohibited such as the detention of a load of counterfeit copper currency. To the Mexican government and people, the most outrageous claims originated from filibuster attempts that became routine in the 1840s when various North Americans and Englishmen would present incredible reclamations for losses and damages after being arrested for conspiracy and set free in San Blas, Mexico.[11]

Since U.S. Minister Anthony Butler had been indiscriminately accumulating claims, it was not easy to resolve the issue immediately. Nevertheless, Ellis demanded immediate reparation and insisted that his government pursue energetic measures.[12] After news of the defeat of the Mexican army at San Jacinto, Secretary of State John Forsyth ordered Ellis to be firm, but to concede a respite before requesting his passports if he did not obtain a favorable response.[13] In spite of the conciliatory attitude of Mexican Foreign Relations Minister Luis G. Cuevas, Ellis attempted to provoke him.[14] When Cuevas asked for details about some of the cases, Ellis requested his passports in December and left. Diplomatic relations remained broken. Although Jackson did not attempt to annex Texas before ending his presidential term, he extended recognition to the Republic of Texas.

The economic depression that confronted the United States inclined the Martin Van Buren government to accept the Mexican offer to submit the claims issue to international arbitration. It was complicated to negotiate the criteria and conditions of the arbitration, but in 1839 it was agreed that the tribunal would include two Mexicans, two North Americans, and a representative from the King of Prussia as an arbiter. After this, the tribunal reduced the amount of U.S. claims from a value that had gone up to 7,585,114 pesos to 2,016,139 pesos.[15] The U.S. government refused to include Mexican claims because of their "national character," which gave way to this unjust procedure. At the conclusion of the first convention's arrangements in 1842, there were new claims,[16] but Minister Waddy Thompson warned that he considered some of them dubious and one so exaggerated that it was difficult for him to support it.[17] A new agreement was signed in 1843 and Mexico began to pay, although not without delays given its delicate financial situation. The total debt was 6,291.604.71 pesos, of which 2,026,139 had been liquidated.

To Mexicans, the disputed issue in relations with the United States continued to be Texas, which had been on the expansionist agenda. British diplomatic pressure and the economic conditions of the nation convinced the majority of Mexican leaders of the advantage in extending recognition to Texas in order to *avoid greater danger*. But continuing Texan incursions and the unpopularity of giving in to the pretensions of "ungrateful Texans" enabled various factions to convert this into an untouchable issue. Nevertheless, at the beginning of 1840, when one of the Texas agents arrived, Minister Juan de Dios Cañedo decided to place the problem before the *Consejo de Gobierno* (Government Council). This body named a commission, headed by Lucas Alamán, to formulate a policy. Alamán elaborated a thoughtful document in which he indicated the evils that come with recognition:

> The commission cannot hide all the difficulties that are going to result…from the recognition of Texas…. The northern frontier is going to be much closer to the center of the Republic and that will facilitate many of the means to encourage contraband; various Northern departments are going to lose direct communication with the Gulf of Mexico and, worst of all, recognition will give a tarnished example to other departments and open the door increasingly to the undertakings of the insatiable Anglosaxon invaders that are not hiding their objective of unlimited extension through the North American continent.

In spite of these problems, the commissioner concluded that a war could not be avoided, but that the Government Council would be wise to consider the following points:

1. That Mexico and the United States enter into negotiations proposed by the British government, by whose mediation they would have the basis for the recognition of Texas.

2. The conditions of this negotiation would be: (1) establishing the boundaries of the new republic; (2) that Texas would maintain its independence without being able to annex itself to another nation; (3) that Mexico be given a financial indemnization which would be applied to its foreign debt; (4) that there be established an indemnization in favor of Mexican landowners in Texas; (5) that there also be established policies to impede Indian attacks into Mexican territory; (6) if possible, to try to have all stipulations come under British guarantee.[18]

Unfortunately for Mexico, its former minister in the United States, Manuel Eduardo Gorostiza, worked to obtain a negative vote and this transferred the decision to the congress. As the rumor filtered to the press, the scandal neutralized all possibility of action. Richard Pakenham, the British minister, commented that Mexico feared the unpopularity of granting recognition which made it difficult to reach any arrangement because of the Texas claim to the Río Grande boundary.[19]

Great Britain recognized the Republic of Texas in 1840 and insisted strongly that the Mexican government also come to an understanding with Texas. Both France and Great Britain wanted to check North American expansionism, which would harm the equilibrium of powers in the New World so they insisted upon recognition of Texas. In a confidential 1841 memorandum for the consideration of the Mexican government Lord George Hamilton Gordon, Count of Aberdeen, offered to guarantee the northern frontier.[20] The Foreign Office began to advise the Mexican government that its stubbornness could endanger other regions, especially California, where North American infiltration increased fear that the Texas experience would be repeated. Nevertheless, it was not easy to overcome the problems created by Texan demands for more territory that now included New Mexico. Although most agreed that the province had been lost, it was difficult to accept the Texas terms presented by the British when the demands arrived accompanied by maritime Texas threats to Gulf of Mexico ports and attempts to conquer New Mexico.

With the increase of expansionist rhetoric in political statements and in the North American press that were reproduced in Mexico, the problem spread. The political agenda was converted into efficient vehicles of information. News about the threat from the north was circulated into the most remote regions. The popular conscience registered every insult from the *tejanos* and *norteamericanos*, limiting the realistic possibilities of a resolution.

In 1842, during his second presidency, Sam Houston decided to carry out annexation. Changing his strategy, Houston requested that an armistice with Mexico be mediated by the British. He never sent this message, but it prompted Lord Aberdeen to conceive a "utopian" plan of triple mediation whereby Great Britain, France and the United States would induce Mexico to extend recognition. Aberdeen later modified his stance, offering Mexico a simple British-French guarantee.[21] Antinio López de Santa Anna never understood clearly the dimensions of the Texas problem and wasted the opportunity to assure British support for Mexico.[22] Internal problems, however, besieged Santa Anna who accepted the armistice request from Houston, which actually gave time to define the conditions for annexation. Although signed, the armistice never became effective because as soon as Houston satisfied his annexation demands with Secretary of State John C. Calhoun, he stopped worrying about war with Mexico.[23]

Under British pressure in November 1844, a month before being removed from power, Santa Anna accepted the conditions for the recognition of Texas.[24] The stipulations enabled British Minister Charles Bankhead to urge the new government of José Joaquin de Herrera to negotiate. In May 1845, the Mexican response was carried by a British agent in Texas onto a French ship. But this was all totally extemporaneous; in July, 1845, the Texas legislature approved the incorporation of the republic to the Union.

James K. Polk undertook expansive measures not only to assure the annexation and security of Texas, but also to incite war between Texas and Mexico. His agent Robert Stockton went to Texas in order to provoke Mexico so that the United States would have to intervene.[25] The rhetoric whined about "resisting invasion" in order to dis-

Antonio Lopez de Santa Anna (1794-1876), President of Mexico. (Special Collections Division, The University of Texas at Arlington Libraries, Arlington, Texas.)

guise the orders sent to the departments of war and navy. While the Texas legislature approved annexation, navy minister George Bancroft notified Commander John Sloat, chief of the naval forces in the Pacific, about relations between Mexico and the United States:

> The Mexican ports on the Pacific are said to be open and defense-less. If you ascertain with certainty that Mexico has declared war against the United States, you will at once possess yourself of the port of San Francisco and blockade or occupy such other ports as your forces may permit.[26]

Bancroft ordered Commodore David Conner, stationed in Pensacola, to take the Mexican ports as a show of force with "perhaps the largest fleet that ever sailed under the American flag" and, in case of war, to take possession of Tampico and, if possible, San Juan de Ulúa, Veracruz. Zachary Taylor received orders to march south, aided by Captain Stockton in the transit of these troops.[27] Buchanan also wrote to Thomas O. Larkin, the U.S. consul at Monterey, California, stating that he did not believe there would be war because it would be possible to purchase Mexican territory. But he established the pol-icy procedures:

> On all proper occasions you should not fail prudently to warn the government and people of California of the danger of such inter-ference [of European powers] to their peace and prosperity; to inspire them with a jealousy of European dominion and to arouse in their bosoms a love of liberty and independence so natural to the American continent—whilst the President will make no effort and use no influence to induce California to become one of the free and independent states of this Union, yet if the people should desire to unite their destiny with ours, they would be received as brethren, whenever this can be done without affording Mexico just cause of complaint.[28]

For his part, Cuevas, the Mexican minister of foreign relations, considered U.S.-Mexican relations broken upon receiving the official notice of the congressional joint resolution concerning the annexation of Texas. This is what former minister José María Bocanegra had warned Mexico about in 1844 and Cuevas notified the North American representative in Mexico City.[29] The North Americans responded by sending a confidential agent, William Parrott, to negotiate with Mexican authorities and James Buchanan announced that:

> the admission of Texas as one of the states of this union, having received the sanction both of the legislative and executive departments of the government is now irrevocably decided, so far as the United States are concerned…. The president nevertheless sincerely regrets that the government of Mexico should have taken offence at these proceedings and he earnestly trusts that it may be disposed to view them in a more favorable light.[30]

The U.S. agent could not gain access to Mexican authorities and asked through the consul if the Mexican government would receive a commissioner. The minister of foreign relations assumed that someone would come to negotiate the reestablishment of an interchange between the two countries and he answered by saying that someone would be received if he would be a commissioner "with full authority …to *arrange*, in a peaceful, reasonable, and decorous manner, the *current dispute*."[31] Charles Bankhead, the British minister in Mexico, wrote to Pakenham, now the British minister in the United States, to ask him to arrange that an adequate person be selected to secure a peaceful accord. Pakenham mentioned to Aberdeen that:

> an amicable settlement of the Texas question will, I fear, have rather an unfavorable effect upon our interests in this part of the world at the moment, I mean with reference to the Oregon Question.[32]

In a separate dispatch, Pakenham emphasized that while Mexicans had been thinking about resolving the Texas problem, the North Americans wanted to obtain more territory. He informed Aberdeen that the United States had been disposed to concede one or two million dollars "for the *arbitrary boundary line already adopted by this country, for the money applied to U.S. claims*" [emphasis added] if "the negotiation should be confined simply to the settlement of the Texas question," so that "*California forms an essential part of the combination.*"[33]

But the Polk administration had been so sure that it would be able to obtain territory in exchange for reparations, that it approved the consent of the Mexican government to send a minister plenipotentiary to carry through its plans. Secretary of State James Buchanan selected John Slidell in spite of the warnings from ex-minister Joel R. Poinsett and the ex-secretary of the legation Benjamin E. Green that Mexico would not receive Slidell with the rank of plenipotentiary; nevertheless, he was given such status.[34] His instructions insisted that "the first subject which will demand your attention is the claims of our citizens on Mexico," without discussing the Texas theme because:

the independence of Texas must be considered a settled fact *and is not to be called into question.* Texas achieved her independence on the plain of San Jacinto in April, 1836.

Neither was Slidell to accept any compensation concerning the Texas boundary since representatives of the region between the Nueces River and Río Grande had participated in the Texas congress, "besides, this portion of the territory was embraced within the limits of ancient Louisiana." The essential part of Slidell's instructions embraced a list of quantities of money to offer for various portions of New Mexico and California territories, insisting that "the possession of the bay and harbor of San Francisco is all important to the United States," assigning twenty million dollars as the maximum amount to offer for their purchase.[35]

Just as Pakenham suspected, the Mexican government waited for a commissioner who might restore relations and determine the Texas issue, while the North Americans considered the Texas issue settled and were only interested in buying territory. United States' interests in California were not new. Since Santa Anna's brief 1836 stay in Washington, Jackson had expressed an interest in purchasing northern California for three-and-a-half million dollars. Descriptions of California published by Alexander Forbes and Eugene Duflot de Maufras hastened desire for the territory and the interest of Secretary

of State Daniel Webster, who was convinced by minister Waddy
Thompson that "Texas has little value compared to California, the
richest land, the most beautiful as well as the healthiest."[36]

The Foreign Office messages about the danger that menaced
California can be summed up by the significance of warnings that
Monterey had been assaulted in 1842, which was carried out by
Commodore Thomas Jones. By 1845 it was no secret that California
was one of Polk's goals[37] and the feeble Mexican military presence in
that province made it seem easy. At the end of 1845, Captain John C.
Frémont appeared in California. In March 1846, he had installed himself near the port of Monterey without permission or passport. When
Frémont received notification from Commander José Castro that he
should leave California, not only did he refuse but Frémont constructed a fortress and raised the U.S. flag.[38]

Since California had a population of barely 24,800 *mexicanos* and
foreigners threatened from all sides, the Mexican government was pes-
simistic about its fate. In congress, some suggested the advantage of
selling it or surrendering it to Great Britain in exchange for its debts to
England. The Mexican minister in London suggested making
California into an independent state endorsed by France and Great
Britain. Private parties also imagined fantastic schemes.[39] Although
Minister Aberdeen was offended by the occupation of California, he
was not inclined to upset the "European balance of power" and tackle
the Oregon question.[40] Aberdeen no longer spoke of guarantees, but
rather offered simple mediation and advised Mexico to abstain at all
costs from declaring war on the United States so that it would "never
have the right to occupy any part of its territory."[41]

The Mexican government was certain that war was inevitable,
fully aware, meanwhile, that it lacked money and weapons, had an
army of barely 30,000 troops, and was clearly incapable of defending
an almost-uninhabited and very extensive border. To make things
worse, by the time General Zachary Taylor crossed the border at the
Nueces River, the monarchist plot elaborated by the Spanish government instigated General Mariano Paredes y Arrillega, backed by the
Reserve Division, to revolt and overthrow President Herrera.[42]

At this precise moment Slidell appeared with inadequate credentials. His presence encouraged the rumor that the Herrera government had decided to "sell Texas and California," which facilitated the Paredes revolt and made it impossible for Mexican officials to receive Slidell. But Polk, in spite of his earnest wish to avoid the expenses and political costs of conflict, began to prepare for a "little war that would justify a durable peace" that would win the coveted Mexican territories. Upon receiving the first dispatches (December 20, 24, 27, and 29, 1846)[43] describing Slidell's difficulties, Polk ordered Taylor, who was now at Corpus Christi, to advance to the Río Grande without informing the public of his provocative order.[44]

For his part, Buchanan instructed Slidell to stay in Mexico to see if the new regime would be more receptive:

[S]hould the Mexican government finally refuse to receive you, then demand passports from the proper authority and return to the United States. It will then become the duty of the President to submit the whole case to Congress and call upon the nation to assert its just rights and avenge its injured honor. In addition to the naval forces already in the Gulf, the frigates *Cumberland*, *Potomac*, and *Raritan* have been ordered to rendezvous before Veracruz as speedily as possible. Should war become inevitable, the President will be prepared to conduct it with vigor.[45]

Mexico's only hope was that the deterioration of relations between Great Britain and the United States would break out into war. But this hope vanished in mid-1846 with the signing of a treaty between Great Britain and the United States. Mexican diplomatic efforts in Mexico as in London centered on gaining some British support, but stumbled against Aberdeen's position, shared by Henry Temple Palmerston, when he took charge of the Foreign Office. Another international aggravation for Mexico was the split in relations declared by French minister Alleye de Cyprey over a minor incident. Cyprey claimed that he had been insulted and demanded an apology and reparations. When he did not get them he broke off diplomatic relations.

Polk very much desired to avoid an expensive war to the point that he approved the insinuations of a Spanish-descended adventurer, Colonel Alexander Atocha, to take advantage of Santa Anna, then exiled in Havana. Although Polk was suspicious of Atocha, he decided to send an agent to interview the ex-president in July, 1846. Santa Anna expressed an interest in signing a treaty and avoiding war, enabling the ex-chief executive to cross the U.S. blockade and return to Mexico.[46] The North American press noted the visit and the news was reported in Mexico. The incident revived suspicions about the conduct of the *general en jefe* of the army, which further weakened the Mexican resolve.

By March, 1846, Taylor had arrived at the mouth of the Río Grande—disputed Mexican territory. This fact did not escape the North American Colonel Ethan Hitchcock, who confessed to his diary:

> *We have not one particle of right to be here* [emphasis added]. Our force is altogether too small for the accomplishment of its errand. It looks as if the government sent a small force on purpose to bring on a war, so as to have a pretext for taking California and as much of this country as it chooses.[47]

The incident Polk sought did not take long. On April 25, an exchange of fire on the Río Grande between soldiers of the two countries resulted in fatalities. Taylor sent a laconic message: "hostilities may now be considered as commenced" which arrived in Washington on May 9. Polk had his declaration of war already prepared. He began by alluding to the reparations, the Mexican refusal to receive Slidell, sent "with powers to adjust every existing difference," to mentioning that Taylor's advance "to the Texas boundary" had been obstructed by the aggressive spirit of Mexican leaders:

> The grievous wrongs perpetrated by Mexico upon our citizens throughout a long period of years remain unredressed; and solemn treaties, pleading her public faith for this redress have been disregarded.... We have tried every effort at reconciliation. The cup of

forbearance has been exhausted, even before the recent information from the frontier of the Del Norte. *But now, after reiterated
menaces, Mexico has passed the boundary of the United States, has
invaded our territory, and shed American blood upon American soil.
She has proclaimed that hostilities have commenced, and that the two
nations are now at war.*[48]

The message was sent to congress on May 11 and approved the
next day. Some congressmen objected that Polk attributed the blame
for war to Mexico, but none dared to oppose the approval of funds to
continue with the conflict. The unjust war of conquest had begun.
When the new Mexican congress met in June, its members simply
acknowledged that a "state of war with the United States" existed.
The constant insults now proceeded from an unscrupulous United
States eager to obtain the desired territory. The same conduct followed after the battles of May 8 and 9 along the Río Grande and indicate the point to which the plans for the war with Mexico bypassed a
simple defense of the long-debated Texas frontier. The result was foreseen and the peace treaty signified the consolidation of the outrage to
Mexico.

* * *

Polk's accusations of Mexican insults and lack of payments were
inaccurate. Still in the middle of great difficulties, the various
Mexican governments complied with the payments and the suspen-
sions were always temporary. The war-like Mexican attitude that
Justin Smith emphasized and that historians Pletcher and Gene Brack
still mention never existed either. From 1837 to 1846, the Mexican
political scene was still dominated by federalist uprisings in such a
way that in spite of Mexican intentions to recapture Texas, the
national governments were subjected to external and internal pressure. Even as the North American invasion began in 1846, the central government had to divert troops to subdue the federalists.[49]

The North American expansionist rhetoric generated an absurd
rhetorical response. Mexico's general debility brought Minister Jose

Maria Bocanegra to lower himself to answering the impertinent actions of the North American Attaché Benjamin Green in 1844. The Mexican governments understood perfectly the impossibility of undertaking war and tried to avoid it. Mexico's weakness made its diplomacy take refuge in international law and justice, a feeble defense against an enemy determined to obtain its territory.

One aspect that cannot be sidestepped is that political instability favored the enemy, and permitted foreign powers to make threats, apply political pressure and intervene in Mexican politics. The most serious meddling was the monarchical conspiracy carried out by Spain which eliminated a natural ally and obtained French-British consent. It was the ultimate effort to stop North American expansionism without risking war.[50] This condemned Mexico to face its forceful neighbor alone. By then everything favored the United States: its dynamism, its natural resources, the possibility of mobilizing volunteers and training them, the existence of an efficient well-armed military led by professional officers, and superior long-range artillery.

That the event was unjust and was caused basically by expansionism seems indisputable. North American peace commissioner Nicholas Trist expressed his conviction of the unjust nature of the event. On February 2, 1848, after many tribulations at the moment of signing the peace treaty, when four signatories were at the point of putting their names on the document, Bernardo Couto, with a grievous voice, turned to Trist and told him, "This has to be a moment of great pride for you but humiliating for us." Trist responded: "We are making peace and this must be our only thought." Much later, in familiar surroundings, Trist commented:

> Could these Mexicans have seen into my heart at that moment, they would have known that *my* feelings of shame as an American was far stronger than theirs could be as Mexicans. For although it would not have done for me to say that in *there*, that was a thing for every right-minded American to be ashamed of, and I *was* ashamed of it, most cordially and intensely ashamed of it. This had been my feelings at all our conferences, and especially at moments

when I had felt it necessary to *insist* upon things which they were adverse to. Had my course at such moments been governed by my conscience as a man and my sense of justice as an individual American, I should have *yielded* in every instance. Nothing prevented my doing so but the conviction that the treaty would then be one which there would be no chance for the acceptance of by our government. My object throughout was not to obtain all that I could, but on the contrary, to make the treaty as exacting as little as possible from Mexico, as well as compatible with its being accepted at home.[51]

NOTES

1. John S. D. Eisenhower, *So Far From God: The U.S. War With Mexico* (New York: Anchor Books, 1990), p. xvii.

2. David Pletcher, *The Diplomacy of Annexation: Texas, Oregon and the Mexican War* (Columbia: University of Missouri Press, 1973).

3. Robert W. Johannsen, *To the Halls of the Montezumas: The Mexican War in the American Imagination* (New York: Oxford University Press, 1985).

4. See Pedro Santoni, *Mexicans at Arms: Puro Federalists and the Politics of War, 1845-1848* (Fort Worth: Texas Christian University Press, 1996) and Josefina Zoraida Vázquez, ed., *México al tiempo de su guerra con Estados Unidos, 1846-1848* (Mexico City: Fondo de Cultura Economica, 1997).

5. Pletcher, *The Diplomacy*, p. 31.

6. Frederick Merk, *Manifest Destiny and Mission in American History: A Reinterpretation* (New York: Knopf, 1963), p. 9-15.

7. Ramón Alcaraz, et al, eds., *Apuntes para la historia de la guerra entre México y los Estados Unidos* (Mexico City: Siglo XXI, 1985, 1991), p. 40.

8. *Don Manuel Eduardo de Gorostiza y la cuestion de Texas* (Mexico City: 1924), pp. 51-59.

9. Forsyth to Ellis, Jan. 29, 1836, in William R. Manning, *Diplomatic Correspondence of the United States: Inter-American Affairs, 1831-1860* (Washington: Carnegie Endowment for International Peace, 1937), vol. 8, p. 38.

10. Ashburham to Palmerston, July 26, 1837, Public Records Office, Foreign Office (hereafter cited as FO), files 50, 107, 141-144. The majority of the claims were considered indefensible. File 50 refers to Mexican items in the Foreign Office.

11. Pakenham to Palmerston, July 5, 1840, FO, 50, 136, 95-102.

12. George L. Rives, *The United States and Mexico, 1821-1848: A History of the Relations Between the Two Countries from the Independence of Mexico to the Close of the War with the United States* (New York: Charles Scribners, 1913), pp. 420-423.

13. James Morton Callahan, *American Foreign Policy in Mexican Relations* (New York: Macmillan, 1932), pp. 92-95; Rives, *The United States*, pp. 424-25.

14. Ashburham to Palmerston, June 2, 1837, FO, 50, 106, 228-230.

15. Francisco de Arrangóiz, *México desde 1808 a 1867* (Mexico City: Editorial Porrua, 1974), p. 308.

16. Waddy Thompson to Daniel Webster, Aug. 16, 1842, in Manning, *Diplomatic Correspondence*, vol. 8, pp. 512-13.

17. Waddy Thompson to Daniel Webster, Nov. 30, 1842, in Manning, *Diplomatic Correspondence*, vol. 8, pp. 523-24: "The first three are all pretty much the same character, as to any negotiation as to them, I have to observe that I have *none of the data upon which to enter into their discussion, except the assertions of the parties...* as to the 4th, the claims of Mr. Parrott, it may be an no doubt is just to some extent, but I cannot forbear to say, *that it is exaggerated to a disgusting degree.* To assert such a claim would subject me and my Government to ridicule if nothing worse.

18. Lucas Alamán, "Dictamen sobre la independencia de Tejas," May 29, 1840, in Lucas Alamán, *Obras: Documentos diversos* (Mexico City: Editorial Jus, 1945), vol. 10, pp. 545-52.

19. Pakenham to Palmerson, April 28, 1840, FO, 50, pp. 134, 148-52. Since 1836, Charles O'Gorman insisted that the Río Grande boundary "would embrace a large extent of territory *not before belonging to Texas.*" O'Gorman to Palmerson, June 21, 1836, FO, 50, 101, 218. The British agent Charles Elliot stated in 1842 that: "It does not seem possible that the Mexicans will be brought to admit the actual Texian demarcation of the western frontier and I *certainly have never discovered upon what former territory the pretention to the line of the río Grande is founded.* What has been said about national geographic limits might equally be said of the Pacific line. In peace, perhaps this government would exercise sound judgement in abandoning any pretention to the country west of the Nueces."

Elliot to Aberdeen, Sept. 15, 1842, Earl of Aberdeen Papers, British Library, vol. 87, p. 31.

20. Confidential Memorandum, May 11, 1841, FO, 50, 145, 187-189.

21. Aberdeen to Pakenham, July 1, 1842, FO, 50, 152, 158-66; Memorandum of April 26, 1842, *Papers of Robert Peel*, British Library, vol. 222, pp. 121-25.

22. Count Aberdeen was preparing a French-British guarantee of the northern Mexican border in exchange for recognition of Texas, thereby jeopardizing the option that it not be annexed to another nation. Aberdeen discussed these issues with the Mexican minister in London on May 29, 1844, and a few days later proposed a similar plan to the Texas minister. Aberdeen to Bankhead, June 3, 1844, FO, 50, 172, 33-36. Memorandum of May 31, 1844, FO, 50, 180, pp. 21-25.

23. Rives, *The United States*, vol. 2, pp. 596-97.

24. Josefina Zoraida Vázquez, "Santa Anna y el reconocimiento de Texas," *Historia Mexicana*, vol. 36, no. 3 (1987), pp. 553-62.

25. Glenn W. Price, *Origins of the War with Mexico: The Polk-Stockton Intrigue* (Austin: University of Texas Press, 1967).

26. Rives, *The United States*, vol. 2, p. 165.

27. Ibid., pp. 164-65.

28. Ibid., p. 167.

29. Bocanegra to Almonte, May 10 and 30, 1844, in Pletcher, *The Diplomacy*, p. 154; Cuevas to Shannon, April 2, 1845, FO, 50, 185, pp. 6-7.

30. Buchanan to Parrot, March 28, 1845, in Carlos Bosch García, *Las reclamaciones, la guerra y la paz* (Mexico City: INAM, 1985), pp. 474-76.

31. De la Peña to Black, Oct. 15, 1845, in Bosch García, *Las reclamaciones*, pp. 613-23.

32. Pakenham to Aberdeen, Nov. 13, 1845, FO, 5, 429, 92-98, and 117-119. File 5 refers to Foreign Office items relating to the United States.

33. Pakenham to Aberdeen, Nov. 13, 1845, FO, 5, 429, 92-98.

34. Pletcher, *Diplomacy*, pp. 278-79.

35. Buchanan to Slidell, Nov. 10, 1845, in Manning, *Diplomatic Correspondence*, vol. 8, pp. 172-82.

36. Thompson to Webster, April 28, 1842, cited by Frank Knapp in "The Mexican Fear of Manifest Destiny in California," *Essays in Mexican History* (Austin: University of Texas Press, 1958), p. 197.

37. "[T]he Mexican War was not the result of the annexation of Texas. The Mexican War was waged for the fulfillment of Polk's designs upon California." See Jesse S. Reeves, *American Diplomacy Under Tyler and Polk* (Baltimore: Johns Hopkins Press,1907), p. 288.

38. Rives, *The United States*, vol. 2, p. 174; Knapp, "The Mexican Fear of Manifest Destiny in California," pp. 192-08.

39. The British consul Erwin Mackintosh conceived obtaining a twenty-year concession for which he would pay ten million pesos to colonize and develop the mines, fisheries and other resources of California.

40. Murphy to Relaciones, May 1, 1845, and Feb. 1, 1846, in Antonio de la Peña y Reyes, *Lord Aberdeen, Texas and California* (Mexico City: Secretaria de Relaciones Exteriores, 1935), pp. 24-26, 62-64.

41. Murphy to Relaciones, Aug. 1, 1845, in de la Peña, *Lord Aberdeen*, pp. 36-38.

42. The plotter behind the conspiracy to put a Spanish prince on a Mexican throne was the Spanish minister in Mexico, Salvador Bermúdez de Castro. Since 1845, the Spanish government approved sums of money for this maneuver. After Paredes took power, Spain initiated contact with the French court and Great Britain to gather their support. Bermúdez de Castro, Memorandum of Feb. 1, 1846, Archivo Histórico Nacional, Madrid, Box 1, Legajo 5869.

43. Manning, *Diplomatic Correspondence*, vol. 8, pp. 785-87, 790-805.

44. Eisenhower, *So Far From God*, pp. 49-50, cites the careful order to Taylor: "It is not designed, in our present relations with Mexico, that you should treat her as an enemy; but should she assume that character by a declaration of war or any open act of hostility towards us, you will not act merely on the defensive, if your relative means enable you to act otherwise.... Texas is now fully incorporated into our union of states, and you are hereby authorized to make a requisition of that State for such of its militia force as may be needed to repel invasion or to secure the country against apprehended invasion." Eisenhower notes that the order violated Article 1 of the Constitution that limits the use of militias to suppress insurrections and repel invasions but not to begin invasions. See also Rives, *The United States*, vol. 2, p. 133.

45. Buchanan to Slidell, Jan. 28, 1846, in Manning, *Diplomatic Correspondence*, vol. 8, pp. 187-88.

46. C. Alan Hutchinson, "Farías and the Return of Santa Anna to Mexico," in *Essays in Mexican History*, p. 187.

47. Ethan Allen Hitchcock, *Fifty Years in Camp and Field: Diary of Major General Ethan Allen Hitchcock* (New York: G.P. Putnam, 1909), p. 213.

48. James D. Richardson, *A Compilation of the Messages and Papers of the Presidents, 1789-1891* (New York: Bureau of National Literature, 1897), vol. 4, pp. 437-43.

49. Federalzist revolts in southern Mexico, Guadalajara and Mazatlán forced Parades to send his most trusted generals and efficient officers with troops to subdue them. General Francisco Pacheco was sent with a division to Guadalajara. In this regard, consult legajo IX/481.3/2230 of the Archivo Histórico de le Secretaría de Defensa Nacional y the correspondence of Pacheco to Parades in carpetas 145 and 147 of the Archivo de Mariana Paredes y Arrillaga in the Benson Latin American Collection of the University of Texas, Austin. Generals Angel Guzmán and Joaquín Rea were sent to fight the insurrection of General Juan Alvarez in the southern area of the State of Mexico. See legajos IX481.3/2196 and 2198 of the Archivo Histórico de la Secretaría de la Defensa and the *informe* of Angel Guzmán to Paredes from Iguala, April 23, 1846, number 232 within carpeta 145, Benson Latin American Collection. The only revolt that could be stopped was one in Mazatlán carried out by General José Ignacio Gutiérrez according to his *informe* from Mazatlán on April 8, 1846, in number 68 of carpeta 145 of the Archivo de Paredes, Benson Latin American Collection.

50. Miguel Soto, *La conspiración monárquica en Mexico, 1845-1846* (Mexico City: EOSA, 1988); Jaime Delgado, *La monarquía en México, 1845-1847* (Mexico City: Editorial Porrua, 1990).

51. Fragment of Virginia Jefferson Trist letter to Mr. [?] Tuckerman, Trist papers, 2104, Southern Historical Collection, University of North Carolina, Chapel Hill. Cited by Robert W. Drexler, *Guilty of Making Peace: Biography of Nicholas P. Trist* (Lanham: University Press of America, 1991), p. 129, and Alejandro Sobarzo, *Deber y conciencia: Nicolas Trist, el negociador norteamericano en la guerra del 1847* (Mexico City: Diana, 1990), p. 233.

4.
"Will the Regiment Stand It?"
The 1st North Carolina Mutinies
at Buena Vista

by Richard Bruce Winders

Any officer or soldier who shall strike his superior officer, or draw or lift up any weapon; or offer any violence against him, being in the execution of his office, on any pretense whatsoever, or shall disobey any lawful command of his superior officer, shall suffer death, or such other punishment as shall, according to the nature of his offense, be inflicted by the sentence of a court-martial.

The Articles of War
Article 9

Politics and war have always gone hand-in-hand. The U.S.-Mexican War of the mid-nineteenth century was no different. The war—its causes, conduct, and consequences—became a battleground in the struggle between the two great parties of Jacksonian America. Most histories describe the fight between Democrats and Whigs in the halls of Congress, usually focusing attention on the Wilmot Proviso and how the bill ensured the slavery issue would become irrevocably linked to the war's outcome. Less known is how Democrats and Whigs fought each other for control of the American military establishment. The nation's reliance on citizen-soldiers, or volunteers, made it impossible to keep politics and patronage out of the camp and field. The stakes were high because voters routinely elected successful military heroes to local, state, and even national office. With the examples of

Washington, Jackson and Harrison before them, Democrats and Whigs vied with one another for positions of command. As the following episode shows, political fighting between volunteers could be just as deadly as any battlefield encounter.[1]

A court of inquiry determined that a mutiny[2] involving three volunteer regiments took place near Saltillo on the night of August 15, 1847. The riot left one dead, one wounded and nearly destroyed several reputations. Military authorities acted quickly to punish the ringleaders and dismissed four volunteers from the service—a lenient sentence in view of their criminal actions. The case ultimately involved James K. Polk, the commander-in-chief of the United States armed forces.[3] The Paine Mutiny, as the affair came to be called, revealed how party politics affected the army during the war with Mexico as Democrats and Whigs battled each other in Congress, the state house, and even in the camps and fields of Mexico.[4]

The units involved in the affair, the 1st North Carolina Infantry,[5] the 1st Virginia Infantry,[6] and the 2nd Mississippi Rifles,[7] were all raised late in the war. Congress had passed a bill on May 11, 1846, to raise 50,000 volunteers, but the men and officers of these regiments missed the first round of inductions. Although North Carolinians eagerly formed companies in expectation of going to war, the War Department mobilized states closest to Mexico, leaving the Tar Heels to wait. Authorization to raise one regiment of infantry finally came in November, 1846, after much of the enthusiasm for the war had cooled. Unlike the earlier volunteer regiments, which had been enlisted for one year, late war volunteers had to agree to serve "for the war." The 1st Virginia and 2nd Mississippi were raised at the same time as the North Carolina unit. Hardship especially dogged the Mississippians, who had to endure serious bouts with measles, influenza and small pox. Disease hit the other two regiments as well, meaning that many officers were often on the sick list and unable to supervise their men. These shaky beginnings, combined with the stark boredom of garrison duty in northern Mexico, created conditions ripe for unrest in the three regiments comprising the only infantry brigade still at Buena Vista.

To Arms! To Arms!

100 Men for the United States Army!

TO THE PATRIOTIC CITIZENS OF HOLMES COUNTY, WHO ARE WILLING TO FIGHT FOR THEIR COUNTRY; AND PARTICULARLY TO THE MEMBERS OF THE "HOLMES COUNTY VOLUNTEER" COMPANY, WHO PLEDGED THEMSELVES TO BE IN READINESS TO MARCH WHEN THE COMPANY WOULD BE ACCEPTED:

FELLOW-CITIZENS AND SOLDIERS:

We are extremely gratified to be able to announce to you, that we have obtained permission from the President of the United States, to organize our company, and also his assurance that, when it is reported to him filled and fully organized, that we will be "Promptly ordered on to the seat of war without the possible intervention of any authority."

So that you see that justice, although sometimes slow is nevertheless sure. Now then, let there be a general rally, to the standard of our beloved country; heed not the insidious whisperings and prophecies of the enemies of Liberty. Let every good, brave and patriotic Citizen, assist in this work; and the ark of American rights will move gloriously forward.

A Recruiting

Rendezvous, has been opened, according to instructions, at the Law Office, of Messrs. Tanneyhill & Given, in the town of Millersburg; where any able-bodied citizen of good character, can enrol his name, and "Go where glory awaits nim."

Let there be a Grand

Rally of the strong arms and stout hearts at this Depot, on SATURDAY next, the 6th inst., at 10 o'clock A. M. when the conditions of the enlistment will be made known.

T. L. HART, Recruiting Officer.

February 1, 1847.

MEANS, PRINTER, MILLERSBURG

The broadside *To Arms! To Arms!* proved a popular recruiting device during the U.S.-Mexican War. Millersburg, Ohio: 1847. (Jenkins Garrett Library, Special Collections Division, The University of Texas at Arlington Libraries, Arlington, Texas.)

The mutiny centered around Robert Treat Paine,[8] the colonel of the 1st North Carolina Infantry. Paine was not a soldier by profession but a politician who had twice served in the North Carolina House of Commons. Volunteers around Saltillo believed that the new colonel was a tyrant whose style of discipline was too strict for citizen-soldiers such as themselves. Colonel Paine struggled all through the summer to bring his regiment up to the standard expected of troops at war. According to one member of Paine's command, "There were none of us [officers] too well informed of our duties, and Colonel Paine, from his actions, appeared to feel the responsibility of bringing the regiment of raw recruits directly into the service, and all his efforts appeared to me to tend towards disciplining his regiment."[9] Another witness reported that, "Considerable difficulty was also experienced in getting the men to keep their clothing, arms, and accoutrements in good order, and their camps well policed."[10] Colonel Paine routinely had to make the rounds in his regiment to make sure the companies were turning out at reveille. Paine demanded that troops under his command obey the *Army Regulations* as well as all orders issued by officers such as himself. At least one observer thought that "discipline and general police of the North Carolina camp, at Buena Vista, resembled the discipline and police of regulars more than any other regiment of volunteers."[11]

Lacking support among his own officers in his effort to bring discipline to his camp, many of whom thought him too severe, Colonel Paine adopted a radical plan to teach a lesson to those men who refused to learn the finer points of soldiering. One day, while discussing how to discipline several members of his regiment who "had frequently been derelict in their duties," one of his officers suggested riding the men on a rail. The talk soon turned to constructing a punishment horse, an unofficial form of punishment sometimes used on regular army posts. Some of these devises even had a head and a tail to complete their equine appearance. Humiliation and intense pain befell any unfortunate soldier ordered to straddle the narrow rail that served as the horse's back. Intent on disciplining his men, an exasperated Paine ordered a carpenter to build a punishment horse and had it placed near his tent.

The appearance of the crude device proved to be the catalyst for turning discontentment into a full-scale mutiny as dissatisfaction over the colonel's plan for discipline spread to the nearby camps of the Virginia and Mississippi regiments.[12] Enlisted men throughout the brigade thought that Paine had overstepped his authority in building the punishment horse. They feared the appearance of the horse might herald a general crack down on rowdy behavior and that their commanders, too, might adopt the detestable instrument. On the night of August 14, 1847, a group of Virginia volunteers descended on Colonel Paine's quarters intending to rid the camp of the horse. The colonel was on Company F's street visiting with Captain William P. Graves, assistant commissary of subsistence, and was not present when the attack occurred. Laughing and jeering, the Virginians placed an old saddle and bridle on the wooden horse, prompting one of them to sit atop the structure while the others picked it up and carried him aloft. At the end of their frolic they pulled the horse apart, scattering the pieces on the ground before returning to their own camp. One Virginia officer later testified, ". . . the reason [the Virginians] determined to destroy it was, because the North Carolinians would not do it themselves, and they would not have the precedent of such punishment established, fearing it might be adopted in their own regiment."[13] Paine complained to Colonel John F. Hamtramck, commander of the Virginia regiment, but the two officers decided it would be impossible to apprehend all the culprits since so many men had participated in the demonstration.[14] Still determined to prove his point, Paine had the pieces of the horse put back together.

Not a single officer or guard of any regiment had attempted to stop the rampage, indicating widespread approval of the mob's action. One of Paine's own officers, Lieutenant George E. B. Singletery[15] was even overheard to say that ". . . it was well enough the horse was torn down by the Virginians, for if they had not done it, [the North Carolinians] would have done it themselves. . . ."[16] Bolstered by the lack of opposition or reprimand, the mob prepared to return to Paine's quarters on the following night (August 15) and finish the job.

Officers in the Virginia camp knew something was afoot but failed to act. Some of their men were overheard to say "We are determined to have the wooden horse," and "We will throw the head into Colonel Fagg's tent, and the tail into Colonel Paine's tent."[17] Another Virginia officer reported hearing one man comment, "We can go on now, I have fixed things with the guard."[18] The Mississippians were also in on the plot with one of the officers, "offering to bet fifty dollars there would be a 'stampede,' or fuss of some kind, in the North Carolina camp that night. . . ."[19]

The trouble began in earnest around nine o'clock when several Virginians hurled rocks at Paine's tent. The colonel, at home this time, braved the hail of stones and left his quarters to see why his guards did not stop the outrage. He found few in his regiment willing to support him: the additional guards he sent for feigned illness and refused to come to his aid. Virtually on his own against an increasingly aggressive mob, Paine confronted his assailants. Armed with a sword and a brace of pistols, he advanced toward the crowd who retreated. Paine called out loudly several times for them to halt, but the mutineers refused to obey his commands and in an insolent tone shouted back, "Go to hell, God damn you!" and "Shoot and be damned." Frustrated, angry, with little other recourse, Paine fired into the crowd. The surprised volunteers fled off into the darkness as one Virginian cried out, "ah, God damn him, he has shot me in the hand." Left behind on the ground, though, was Private A. H. Bradly, a member of Lieutenant Josiah Pender's company. Driven to desperation, Paine had faced the mutineers and had single-handedly driven them away but had mortally wounded one of his own men.[20]

The sound of gunfire immediately brought Paine's superiors into the North Carolinian's camp. The incident had been reported to Brigadier General Caleb Cushing[21] who sped to the scene with his staff to assist the embattled colonel. Cushing, the brigade's commander, expressed fear that Colonel Paine was still in danger and tried to convince him to leave the area for his own safety. Brigadier General John E. Wool,[22] the overall commander of the troops in the Saltillo area, quickly arrived with his own staff and a detachment of regulars

A lithograph of Major General John E. Wool. Published about 1850. (Mexican War
Graphics Collection, Special Collections Division, The University of Texas at Arlington
Libraries, Arlington, Texas.)

and ordered Paine to accompany him back to headquarters. Paine complied but shortly thereafter returned to camp. Determined to sleep in his own tent, he retired around one o'clock and experienced no further trouble that night.[23]

The morning brought a new challenge to Paine, who found a note on his adjutant's desk calling on him to resign his commission. The petition read, "Sir: We, officers of the North Carolina regiment of volunteers, believing that it is essential to the quiet and harmony of our regiment, request that you will surrender the commission you now hold."[24] The message had been "written by Lieut. [Josiah S.] Pender, & signed by every Company officer save two."[25] Paine took the impertinent demand to General Wool who denounced the continuing state of mutiny and issued an order summarily dismissing four volunteers from the service who had played prominent roles in the affair. The censured men included three from Paine's regiment, Lieutenant Singletery, Lieutenant Pender,[26] and Private Jason Hunter[27] as well as a Virginian, Private Thomas King.[28] The general suspected that Singletery and Pender were ringleaders in the affair, as evidenced by their names at the top of the list calling for Paine's resignation.[29] Hunter, a member of Pender's company, encouraged others in the regiment to refuse to turn out for guard duty when called by Paine.[30] King had been the man in the crowd wounded in the hand.[31]

General Wool threatened further disciplinary actions, including the dismissal of every officer who had signed the petition. Paine pleaded with him to allow his officers time to reconsider. General Cushing spoke with the men at Paine's request and by the evening of August 17, all had requested that their names be stricken from the list. One mass retraction read, "We, the undersigned, certify on honor that we had no mutinous intentions in signing the 'request' sent to Colonel R. T. Paine, of the North Carolina regiment volunteers, on the 16th inst., and respectfully desire that our names shall be stricken from that list."[32] Colonel Paine observed a change in his men as they lifted their caps when he passed as if making amends for their misdeeds.[33] General Wool ordered the camp of the 1st North Carolina moved several miles to Arispa's Mill to remove it from the influence of the other volunteers at Buena Vista.[34] Wool's quick action and Paine's resolve to stay at the head of his regiment had quelled the mutiny, and a semblance of order returned to Saltillo.

The principle parties in the affair—Colonel Paine and the conspirators—all desperately wanted to clear their tarnished reputations and prove that their actions had been justified. General Wool immediately notified his superior in Monterrey, Major General Zachary Taylor,[35] of the failed mutiny and the dismissal of the ringleaders. Taylor wrote back saying that the incident had been "the most disgraceful and cowardly occurrence which [had] taken place since the commencement of the present war." He approved the dismissals, voicing the opinion that "The prompt measures you have taken to put down the [mutiny] . . . will restore a proper state of discipline in that corps." He concurred that Colonel Paine had performed his duty in a "soldierly manner," thereby officially lifting any cloud of suspicion still lingering over the beleaguered colonel.[36]

Singletery and Pender also contacted Taylor but to no avail. Both officers had been ordered to leave Saltillo on the night of August 16, 1847, and faced "arrest and imprisonment if found in camp."[37] Pender, who had received permission to remain in Saltillo to care for his gravely ill cousin, Captain Solomon Pender, an assistant quartermaster of volunteers, further hurt his case when military officials determined he was more concerned with gathering evidence to use in his defense than actually aiding his dying relative.[38] Taylor upheld Wool's decision and Singletery and Pender were ordered to leave Mexico.[39]

The two cashiered officers were not without their supporters. Three officers of Singletery's company signed a statement claiming that the lieutenant had not participated in the mutiny and that he even had rallied his company to aid Colonel Paine.[40] Twenty officers from the North Carolina regiment swore that Lieutenant Singletery had not induced them to sign the petition calling for Paine's resignation.[41] Thirty officers from the 2nd Mississippi Rifles pressed the matter even further when they sent a letter expressing their disapproval of Wool's actions directly to a high ranking civilian official in Polk's administration, Secretary of Treasury Robert J. Walker.[42] The Mississippians raised several points in their letter. First, according to Article 11 of the Articles of War no officer could be dismissed from the service except by order of the president, or by sentence of a court-martial. Thus, they contended that Wool's actions had been illegal. Second, the accused officers and enlisted men had been denied a hearing at which they could have offered a defense. And last, as volunteers were state troops, the Mississippians questioned the right of any federal official—including the president—to revoke the commission of volunteer officers. These officers hoped Secretary Walker would take their concerns to the president.[43]

Military jurisprudence already insured Polk's involvement in the matter. According to the Articles of War, any case concerning the death penalty or the dismissal of a commissioned officer was automatically "transmitted to the Secretary of War, [and] laid before the President of the United States for his confirmation or disapproval."[44] News of the mutiny and the subsequent dismissals reached Washington in October. So did Lieutenants Pender and Singletery who wanted to present their version of the mutiny in person. Although it is unclear whether they actually met with either Secretary of War William L. Marcy[45] or the president, Pender laid out their grievances in several pointed notes critical of Paine and Wool. Polk sided with the two volunteer officers and, acting with surprising speed, he struck down Wool's ruling and ordered all four of the dismissed men back to duty.[46] The news stunned military officials in Mexico.

Polk claimed that he based his decision on the Articles of War. According to these regulations, officers and men accused of a crime must have their cases heard before a military court where the prisoner and his council could mount a defense against the charges. The president, through Secretary Marcy, declared that Wool had acted unlawfully and had violated the dismissed volunteers' rights.[47] Wool defended his actions to Marcy, saying "I cannot but believe that the officers, as well as the two men in question, were justly and necessarily discharged from the service" and predicted that discipline in the regiment, which had improved, would be harmed if the dismissed men were allowed to return.[48] In dismissing the men, Wool had acted under authority granted him by Winfield Scott, general-in-chief of the army.[49] Nearly a year before the mutiny occurred, Scott had foreseen that instances would arise deep in enemy territory that demanded immediate action by commanders far from the nation's capital. He informed Wool, "You may . . . grant discharges from the service of the United States, 'honorable,' or otherwise . . . upon the presentation of such circumstances as may appear to you of grave interest to the officers themselves, or to the public service."[50] What seemed like a logical idea to Scott and Wool was deemed illegal by Polk and Marcy.

Marcy, when informing Taylor of the president's decision, stated that Polk did not intend for Pender, Singletery and the two enlisted men to go unpunished if in fact they had committed a crime. He announced to the general, "To the end that full information may be obtained in relation to the alleged mutiny and the homicide, which appears to have resulted from it, the President directs you to institute a court of inquiry to investigate all the facts and circumstances of the transactions alluded to, and desires that the proceedings of the court may be forwarded, at your earliest convenience, to this department."[51] Taylor, however, left Mexico in November on a leave of absence. He discussed the Paine Mutiny with an acquaintance on the way home who reported that Taylor "sustained Gen. Wool in all his proceeding consequent upon it [and] expressed his disapprobation of the President's course in reinstating Pender [saying] that he considered Col. Paine as one of the best officers sent to Mexico."[52] With Old Rough and Ready gone from the scene, Wool suddenly learned that the duty of convening an inquiry fell to him in his capacity as the newly appointed commander in northern Mexico. After a brief flurry of letters to the War Department in which he protested the reversal of his decision and the call for an official hearing, Wool directed a court of inquiry to assemble at Saltillo on January 26, 1848.[53]

The court took fifty-eight days to hear the evidence and render its decision. Sitting on the case were Colonel Robert E. Temple,[54] Colonel John W. Tibbatts,[55] Major Lewis Cass, Jr.,[56] and Captain

James H. Prentiss.[57] Colonel Temple presided over the hearing while Captain Prentiss acted as judge advocate[58] and recorder. A parade of enlisted men and officers took the stand throughout the hearing to relate events before, during and after the mutiny. Paine's backers described him as a capable commander whose unappreciative regiment had forced him to resort to violence in order to quell a mutiny and protect his own life. Singletery's and Pender's friends painted a much different picture of the colonel: Paine was a martinet who cursed and struck his own men. After sitting for a month in Saltillo, the court moved to Monterrey to hear the testimony of General Wool. Upon deliberation, the members of the court determined (1) that a mutiny had taken place, (2) that Colonel Paine had acted in the line of duty when he killed one man and wounded another, and (3) that General Wool had acted solely for the public good when he ordered the four men dismissed from the service. On April 12, 1848, after having announced its findings, the court adjourned.[59]

The transcripts of the case indicate several factors contributed to the mutiny at Saltillo. First, the North Carolinians believed Paine treated them in a tyrannical and demeaning manner.[60] Several of his officers had forwarded a letter to General Taylor on August 7 in which they complained about Paine's behavior as colonel.[61] Some of these officers apparently even planned to ask for Paine's resignation weeks prior to the destruction of the punishment horse and the death of Private Bradly.[62] Both Singletery and Pender bore private grudges against Paine. Paine had placed Singletery, only twenty-years-old at the time of the incident, under arrest on several occasions for dereliction of duty.[63] Pender, who had attended West Point for a short time and believed himself well qualified to command, found his path to promotion blocked by Paine, who refused to schedule an election to fill the vacant captaincy that existed in his company.[64] Hurt pride and blocked ambition played a role in the mutiny.

More importantly, though, the evidence presented revealed that party politics played a significant role in the disorder. North Carolina's governor, William A. Graham[65] had sown the seeds of discord months before by his appointment of Paine as colonel. It had become an accepted practice in the United States for the men (or at least the officers) of a volunteer regiment to elect their colonel, lieutenant colonel and major. Graham broke this tradition by dispensing with an election and naming the field officers himself. The problem was that Graham, a Whig, appointed two prominent Whig politicians to command the regiment. Colonel Paine was a member of the North Carolina House of Commons while Lieutenant Colonel John A. Fagg[66] had once held a seat in the General Assembly. One North Carolinian, Thomas Ruffins, painted an amusing image of one of the newly appointed field officers:

> With regards to your enquiries [sic] to Col. Fagg's military character and his character as a gentleman, I am really at a loss to give you a satisfactory answer. I never knew him and scarcely ever heard of the man, until I served in the Legislature with him two years ago. Whether or not he is skilled in military tactics or is renowned for warlike exploits I am wholly ignorant, the most I know or can say of him in that line is, that he is a very *belly cose* looking man and to all appearances could swallow a half dozen small Mexicans without apparently being much inconvenienced by the meal. He is certainly a very rude illiterate man and has evidently not been associated too much with genteel society; to do him justice however, he is what most of his acquaintances call a clever good sort of fellow, who will do well enough in his proper place but out of place won't do at all.[67]

The intent was clearly to give the impression to Ruffin's reader that Graham's choices were unfit to command.

The appointment of Paine, Fagg, and Monfort S. Stokes set off a firestorm in the state's Democratic presses as Graham's opponents charged that he had abused his patronage power by awarding the coveted positions to his party.[68] *The North Carolina Standard* posed the question to its readers, *"Will the Regiment stand it?"* The paper's editors provided their own answer, "We think not."[69] It mattered little to critics that Fagg had been recommended for his position by several leading Democrats or that Stokes,[70] a Democrat, had been appointed major. The leading contender for the position of colonel had been Louis D. Wilson,[71] a popular Democratic politician, but Graham passed him over in making his selection. One editorial in the *Tarborough Press* lamented ". . . the grossest injustice has been done the feelings of those noble Democrats, who have volunteered to serve their country. . . ."[72] *The North Carolina Standard* proclaimed, "Wilson is a Democrat. He may become a formidable candidate of Governor. He may gain laurels in Mexico. Such were the mean feelings and low calculations which have influenced Governor Graham. For shame! For shame!"[73]

Testimony presented at the inquiry makes it clear that staunch Democrats like Pender, who one editor claimed comprised two-thirds of the regiment, still had not recognized Paine as the legitimate commander of the regiment at the time of the mutiny.[74] In a letter to Polk *written shortly before the mutiny*, Pender complained of Paine's appointment, telling the president:

> State laws provided that the selection of field officers should be made by the regiment, but after the regiment had been completed our whig legislature took the selection from an entire democratic regiment, and gave the right of appointment to a whig governor, contrary to the wishes of nine-tenths of the regiment. . . .[75]

Paine's voting record as a Whig made him unacceptable to many Democrats in his regiment. In fact, a company raised for the regiment by Captain Greene Washington Caldwell refused to serve under Paine and joined the 3rd U.S. Dragoons instead.[76] The reason for the uproar was that the colonel, while a state legislator, had supported wording in an appropriation bill for the new regiment that blamed the war on the president and his Democratic administration. Pender claimed in both his letter to Polk and his testimony at the inquiry that Democrats disliked the fact that Paine seemed to oppose the war: "From the course he pursued in the legislature, and the opinions he there expressed, [the officers] could not see how he could take command of the regiment."[77] Pender also made sure Polk knew that Paine had "not only voted for, but supported with his utmost ability, that abominable preamble [which declared] . . . that the *existing war* with Mexico was brought about by the executive, [and] that it was unjust."[78] Pender hoped party loyalty would sway Polk to his side and if other cases involving disputes between Whig and Democratic officers is any indication, it did. More than fifty years later one veteran Tar Heel recalled, "It was thought [at the time] that on account of political matters the President reinstated Pender and Singletery."[79]

The Democratic press in North Carolina had been instrumental in driving a wedge between Paine and his regiment. One witness at the inquiry claimed that

> The Democratic papers of North Carolina have been generally denunciatory of the course of Colonel Paine.... I have seen some articles which were calculated to do injury to the discipline of the regiment.... I believe these articles did an injury to the regiment by keeping up an excitement on matters which were discussed therein. Frequently, two or three month's [later] accounts would return to the regiment of occurrences in the regiment which had long been passed over or forgotten.[80]

Another witness at the inquiry, who was asked if partisan newspapers ever made their way to the regiment, stated "Many copies of all these papers have been received by officers and men of the regiment."[81] Still another testified that "trifling" incidents, long forgotten by the regiment, were often "magnified into hideous monsters" in newspaper from home. He even reported that one story supposedly called Paine *"an old Whig rascal"* and suggested he be shot.[82] An officer loyal to Paine described the unenviable position in which the colonel found himself, saying "The whig editors of newspapers condemn the war, and preach to the people the distress and suffering of the soldiers. The democrats, to balance accounts, accuse the colonel of a want of judgment, tyranny, and cruelty."[83] Surely any man would have had difficulty commanding a regiment of unruly volunteers under these circumstances.

Colonel Paine obviously demanded much of his regiment. Other volunteers, however, had demanding commanders, too, but did not plot to overthrow them. The question must be asked, why did troops camped near Saltillo revolt on those two nights in August 1847? The answer lies in the division of the North Carolina regiment into hostile political factions. Dissatisfied Democratic elements within Paine's regiment—led by Pender and Singletery—fostered the notion within their brigade that their Whig colonel was a petty tyrant and a threat to all volunteers who came within his reach. Having created an atmosphere conducive to mutiny, they stepped back and allowed the riot to occur. Rescued from their punishment by President Polk, the mutinous Pender and Singletery should have appeared before a court-martial instead of a court of inquiry. On the surface, the Paine Mutiny appears to be just another case of rowdy volunteers run amok. Closer examination, however, reveals it to be much more. Historians of the war should note that two battles took place at Buena Vista during the war in Mexico—one between Taylor and Santa Anna, and the other between Democrats and Whigs.

NOTES

1. For a detailed study, see Richard Bruce Winders, *Mr. Polk's Army: The Military Establishment in the Mexican War* (College Station: Texas A&M University Press, 1997).

2. Henry L. Scott, *Military Dictionary: Comprising the Technical Definitions; Information On Raising and Keeping Troops: Actual Service, including Makeshift and improved Matériel; And Law, Government, Relation, and Administration Relating to Land Forces* (New York: D. Van Nostrand, 1864; reprint ed., Yuma, Arizona: Fort Yuma Press, 1984), p. 428; Articles of War, Article 9, in *General Regulations for the Army, 1847* (Washington, D.C.: J. and G. S. Gideon, 1847), p. 2 of appendix.

3. James Knox Polk (1795-1849) of Tennessee had been Andrew Jackson's political protégé and as Speaker of the House helped pass key Democratic legislation. He later returned to his home state to run for governor: he won the seat but failed to hold on to it in the subsequent election. He became the first "dark horse" candidate when he came out of retirement in 1844 to accept his party's nomination as president. With his victory, he assumed the leadership of the Democratic Party shortly before the war.

4. For documents containing the particulars of the Paine Mutiny, see U.S. Congress, Senate, *Message from the President of the United States In Answer to a resolution of the Senate, calling for the proceedings of the court of inquiry convened at Saltillo, Mexico, January 12, 1848, for the purpose of obtaining full information relative to an alleged mutiny at Buena Vista, about the 15th August, 1847*, 30th Cong., 1st sess., Executive Document No. 62; U.S. Congress, House, *Message from the President of the United States, Transmitting a report from the Secretary of War, relative to the dismissal from the public service of J. S. Pender and G. E. B. Singletery, in compliance with a resolution of the House of Representatives of the 17th July, 1848*, 30th cong., 1st sess., Executive Document No. 78. Two first-hand accounts are also in George Winston Smith and Charles Judah, eds., *Chronicles of the Gringos: The U.S. Army in the Mexican War, Accounts of Eyewitnesses and Combatants* (Albuquerque: University of New Mexico Press, 1968), pp. 424-31. Both the Senate and House documents contain a transcript of the court of inquiry held to investigate the incident. Numerous North Carolina newspapers carried accounts of the affair, including *The Carolina Watchman*, Salisbury, North Carolina, October 7, 1847; *The Raleigh Star and North Carolina Gazette*, Raleigh, North Carolina, September 22, September 29, and October 6, 1847; *The Hillsbourgh Recorder*, Hillsbourgh, North Carolina, September 30, and October 7, 1847.

5. U.S. Congress, House, *Military Forces Employed in the Mexican War: Letter from the Secretary of war Transmitting, Information in answer to a resolution of the House, of July 31, 1848, relative to the military forces employed in the late war with Mexico.* 1st Cong., 1st sess., Executive Document No. 24, p. 22b; Adjutant General, *Roster of North Carolina Troops in the War with Mexico* (Raleigh: Josephus Daniels, State Printer and Binder, 1887). For histories of the 1st North Carolina Infantry, see Lee A. Wallace, "Raising a Volunteer Regiment for Mexico, 1846-1847," *North Carolina Historical Review*, vol. 35 (1958), pp. 20-33, and "North Carolina in the War with Mexico" (M.A. thesis, University of North Carolina at Chapel Hill, 1950); William S. Hoffman, *North Carolina in the Mexican War, 1846-1848* (Raleigh: State Department of Archives and History, 1963); *Charlotte Daily Observer* (Charlotte, North Carolina), January 6, 1902.

6. House, *Military Forces Employed in the Mexican War*, p. 22b. For a history of this regiment, see Lee A. Wallace, Jr., "The First Regiment of Virginia Volunteers, 1846-1848," *Virginia Magazine of History and Biography*, vol. 77 (1969), pp. 46-77.

7. House, *Military Forces Employed in the Mexican War*, p. 22c. For a history of this regiment, see Richard Bruce Winders, "The Role of the Mississippi Volunteers in Northern Mexico, 1846-1848" (M.A. thesis, University of Texas at Arlington, 1990), Chapters 11-13.

8. J. G. De Roulhac Hamilton, ed., *The Papers of William Alexander Graham: Volume 3, 1845-1850*, 7 vols. (Raleigh: State Department of Archives and History, 1960), p. 139. Robert Treat Paine (1812-1872), a resident of Chowan, North Carolina, served in the House of Commons from 1838-1840 and 1844-1847 as a Whig. He moved his family to Texas just prior to the Civil War.

9. Senate Ex. Doc. No. 62, p. 75.

10. Ibid., p. 68.

11. Ibid., p. 106.

12. Senate Ex. Doc. No. 62, pp. 23-24; *Wilmington Journal* (Wilmington, North Carolina) September 24, 1847; *Charlotte Daily Observer*, January 6, 1902. When news of the mutiny reached North Carolina, the *Tarborough Press* reported the incident, saying "Col. Paine had been very rigorous in his punishment, and had finally erected a wooden horse for his men to ride (a disgraceful punishment, known in the army). This roused the indignation of his own troops, both officers and men; and brought down sneers and jibes of the Virginian and Mississippi Regiments, encamped near by." The story was reprinted in the *Wilmington Journal*.

13. Senate Ex. Doc. No. 62, p. 162.

14. Ibid., p. 24.

15. Adjutant General, *Roster of North Carolina Troops in the War with Mexico*, p. 30; *Charlotte Daily Observer*, January 6, 1902. Singletery belonged to Company H. Popular with his men, he was elected captain on July 29, 1848, just prior to the regiment's disbandment. Singletery's name appears as "Singletary" in some sources.

16. Senate Ex. Doc. No. 62, p. 87; *Charlotte Daily Observer*, January 6, 1902.

17. Senate Ex. Doc. No. 62, p. 161.

18. Ibid., p. 96.

19. Ibid., p. 115.

20. Senate Ex. Doc. No. 62, pp. 6, 7, 14-21, 45, 58, 65, 90, 91, 116, 201-204; Smith and Judah, eds., *Chronicles of the Gringos*, pp. 425-28; *Charlotte Daily Observer*, January 6, 1902. Friends claimed that Bradly had gone to visit a sick friend and was returning to his tent when shot.

21. Claude M. Fuess, *The Life of Caleb Cushing*, 2 vols. (New York: Harcourt, Brace, and Company, 1923), vol. 2, pp. 3-81; Smith and Judah, eds., *Chronicles of the Gringos*, p. 428; Senate Ex. Doc. No. 62, pp. 38, 75. Massachusetts native Caleb

Cushing (1800-1879) was a prominent Democratic politician at the time of the war who had held both state and national offices. Cushing resigned his position as colonel of the 1st Massachusetts Infantry (another late war regiment) upon being appointed a brigadier general of volunteers by Polk. Cushing was stationed near Saltillo at the time of the mutiny but afterwards was ordered to join Scott in central Mexico. He resumed his political career at the end of the war.

22. Francis B. Heitman, *Historical Register and Dictionary of the United States Army, From Its Organization, September 29, 1789, to March 2, 1903*, 2 vols. (Washington: Government Printing Office, 1903; Gaithersburg, Maryland: Olde Soldiers Book, Inc., 1988), vol.1, pp. 1059-1060; Milo Milton Quaife, ed., *The Diary of James K. Polk During His Presidency, 1845 to 1849*, 4 vols. (Chicago: A. C. McClurg & Company, 1910), vol. 1, p. 418, vol. 2, p. 431. New Yorker John Ellis Wool (1784-1869) distinguished himself as an officer of action and intelligence in the War of 1812. A career soldier, Wool received his appointment as brigadier general in 1841. Ordered at the start of the war to occupy Chihuahua, he led a mixed column of regulars and volunteers from San Antonio into northern Mexico. The War Department aborted the mission before he reached Chihuahua, however, and instructed him instead to link his forces with those of General Zachary Taylor. Wool was second-in-command at the battle of Buena Vista fought on February 22-23, 1847. He became the overall commander of troops in the Saltillo area upon Taylor's removal to Monterrey. Volunteers who served under him thought he was a strict commander. Wool fell into disfavor with Polk and Marcy who thought him slow, unimaginative and bound by tradition.

23. Smith and Judah, eds., *Chronicles of the Gringos*, pp. 428-429; Senate Ex. Doc. No. 62, pp. 20-21, 203-204.

24. Senate Ex. Doc. No. 62, pp. 191-192.

25. Smith and Judah, eds., *Chronicles of the Gringos*, p. 429; *Charlotte Daily Observer*, January 6, 1902; *Carolina Watchman*, September 23, 1847.

26. Heitman, *Historical Register*, vol. 2, p. 60; Charles N. Branham, ed., *Register of Graduates and Former Cadets of the United States Military Academy* (n.p.: West Point Alumni Foundation, Inc., 1964), p. 226; Senate Ex. Doc. No. 62, p. 37. Josiah S. Pender entered the United States Military Academy in 1835 but failed to complete the course of instruction. Pender wrote President Polk during the period leading up to the mutiny to say that he wished to remain in the volunteer service, "having received a penchant for military life at West Point." Said Lieutenant Singletery of Pender's training, "At the formation of the regiment, he was thought to have some considerable advantage over the rest of the officers of the regiment, as he had been some time at West Point."

27. House Ex. Doc. No. 78, p. 7; Senate Ex. Doc. No. 62, p. 16.

28. House Ex. Doc. No. 78, p. 7; Wallace, "The First Regiment of Virginia Volunteers," p. 67.

29. Senate Ex. Doc. No. 62, p. 160.

30. Ibid., p. 16

31. Ibid., p. 91.

32. Ibid., pp. 192-93.

33. Smith and Judah, eds., *Chronicles of the Gringos*, p. 429.

34. Ibid., pp. 30, 123.

35 Heitman, *Historical Register*, vol. 1, p. 949. A native Virginian, Zachary Taylor grew up in the Kentucky countryside near Louisville. A captain in the regular army during the war of 1812, Taylor earned a reputation as a dependable officer. As colonel of the 1st U.S. Infantry, Taylor won a brevet to brigadier general for his attack on the Seminoles at Lake Okeechobee on Christmas Day, 1837. Chosen by the War Department to command the Army of Observation prior to the outbreak of the Mexican War, Taylor found himself at the head of the American Army on the Río Grande when the war began. His victories over the Mexicans at Palo Alto and Resaca de la Palma (May 8 and 9, 1846) earned him a promotion to major general while his success at Monterrey (September 21-24, 1846) and Buena Vista (February 22-23, 1847) won him gold medals from Congress. His battles made him attractive to the Whigs, who courted the general and made him their candidate in the presidential election of 1848. Taylor and Polk disliked each other and throughout the war their rocky relationship reflected partisan politics.

36. Senate Ex. Doc. No. 62, p. 213.

37. House Ex. Doc. No. 78., p. 14.

38. Senate Ex. Doc. No. 62, p. 46.

39. Ibid., pp. 33, 45-47, 98-99; House Ex. Doc. No. 78, p. 7.

40. Senate Ex. Doc. No. 62, pp. 210-11.

41. Ibid., pp. 211-12.

42. House Ex. Doc. No. 78, pp. 7-10; J. Franklin Jameson and J. W. Buel, eds, *Encyclopedic Dictionary of American Reference*, 2 vols. (n.p.: C. R. Graham, 1901), vol. 2, p. 342. Polk selected Robert James Walker (1801-1869), Democratic sena-

tor from Mississippi from 1836 to 1845, as secretary of treasury. Walker authored a tariff bill which bore his name that substantially lowered the tax on many imports.

43. House Ex. Doc., pp. 8-10.

44. Articles of War, Article 65, in *General Regulations, 1847*, p. 13 of appendix.

45. Jameson and Buel, eds, *Encyclopedic Dictionary of American Reference*, vol. 1, pp. 426-27. Democrat William Learned Marcy (1786-1857) was active in state and national politics. He held the posts of New York comptroller (1823-1829), New York associate supreme court justice (1829-1831), U.S. senator (1831-1832), New York governor (1833-1839), secretary of war (1845-1849), and secretary of state (1853-1857). Marcy perhaps is remembered best for his 1832 speech regarding the spoils system when he remarked, "to the victor belongs the spoils." Polk assisted Marcy in running his department throughout the war.

46. Senate Ex. Doc. No. 62, pp. 3-4.

47. Articles of War, Articles 64-90, in *General Regulations, 1847*, pp. 12-17 of appendix.

48. House Ex. Doc. No. 78, pp. 15-16.

49. Heitman, *Historical Register*, vol. 1, p. 870. A native of Virginia, Winfield Scott (1786-1866) dominated the U.S. military for more than fifty years. Only a captain when the war of 1812 began, Scott proved to be a brave and energetic officer who outshone his inept superiors. Raised to the rank of brigadier general, he quickly trained his brigade to the level of British regulars, whom he bested at the battles of Chippewa and Lundy's Lane. Promoted to major general at the end of the war, young Scott still had a lifetime of service to give to his country. In 1841, Scott assumed the position of commanding general of the army. His most unflattering quality was his penchant for quarreling with his fellow officers and superiors, a trait that earned him many bitter enemies. Polk disliked the Whig general, who had political aspirations, and only sent him to Mexico when he could find no way to supersede him. Polk ultimately recalled Scott from Mexico—once the Mexican capital had been secured—and replaced him with William Orlando Butler, a Democratic appointee to the army. Despite Scott's personal flaws, he undoubtedly was the premier military man of his day.

50. Senate Ex. Doc. No. 62, pp. 166, 167, 212-213; House Ex. Doc. No. 78, pp. 15-16.

51. Senate Ex. Doc. No. 62, pp. 2-3.

52. Hamilton, ed., *Papers of William A. Graham*, vol. 3, pp. 211-12, 236.

53. House Ex. Doc. No. 78, pp. 5-7, 14-16, 18-23; Articles of War, Articles 92-93, in *General Regulations, 1847*, pp. 18-19 of appendix. The correspondence between Wool and March is contained only in the House Document.

54. Heitman, *Historical Register*, vol. 1, p. 950. A native of Vermont, Robert Emmet Temple (?-1854) graduated in 1824 from the United States Military Academy fourth in his class. He resigned from the army in 1839. Temple was appointed colonel of the 10th U.S. Infantry, one of the temporary regiments of regulars authorized under the Ten Regiment Bill of February 11, 1847.

55. Heitman, *Historical Register*, vol. 1, p. 960; William B. Cooke, *Speech of William M. Cooke, of Tennessee, In a Review of the War, Its Costs, and Executive Patronage; Delivered in the House of Representatives of the United States, May 18, 1848* (Washington: J. and G. S. Gideon, Printers, 1848), p. 12. Kentuckian John Wollistan Tibbatts (?-1895), was commissioned colonel of the 13th U.S. Infantry, a temporary regiment authorized under the Ten Regiment Bill. Tibbatts was a member of the Kentucky delegation to the 1844 Democratic Convention that nominated Polk for president.

56. Heitman, *Historical Register*, vol. 1, p. 289. Lewis Cass, Jr. (1814-1878), was appointed major of the 3rd U.S. Dragoons, a temporary regiment authorized under the Ten Regiment Bill. His father was Lewis Cass, Sr., prominent Democratic politician and unsuccessful candidate for president in 1848 on the Democratic ticket.

57. Heitman, *Historical Register*, vol. 1, p. 805. James Henry Prentiss (?-1848) graduated in 1826 from the United States Military Academy twelfth in his class. At the time of the inquiry he was a captain in the 1st U.S. Artillery.

58. Scott, *Military Dictionary*, p. 203; Articles of War, Article 69, in *General Regulations, 1847*, pp. 13-14 of appendix. Prentiss' duties were both prosecutor and defense attorney. No similar office exists in civil proceedings. The judge advocate "shall prosecute in the name of the United States, but so far consider himself as counsel for the prisoner, after the said prisoner shall have made his plea, as to object to any leading question to any witness, or any question to the prisoner, the answer to which might criminate [sic] himself." He also administered the oath to each witness who took the stand.

59. Senate Ex. Doc. 62, pp. 5, 165, 187-189; Hamilton, ed., *The Papers of William A. Graham*, vol. 3, p. 236.

60. Senate Ex. Doc. No. 62, pp. 49, 55, 68-69.

61. Ibid., pp. 193-94.

62. Ibid., p. 51.

63. Ibid., pp. 34-35.

64. Ibid., pp. 38, 82.

65. Beth G. Crabtree, *North Carolina Governors, 1585-1974* (Raleigh: Department of Archives and History, Department of Cultural Resources, 1974), pp. 84-85. William Alexander Graham (1804-1875) served in the North Carolina legislature and the U.S. Senate before being elected governor in 1845. He was an ardent Whig who believed in state-backed education. As secretary of the navy under Millard Fillmore, Graham signed the orders sending Commodore Matthew Perry to Japan. In 1852, the Whigs selected Graham as their vice presidential candidate to back Winfield Scott in his unsuccessful run for the White House. Graham supported the Confederacy once his state left the Union in 1861.

66. Hamilton, ed., *The Papers of William A. Graham*, vol. 3, p. 161. John A. Fagg (1807-1888) was a Whig member of the North Carolina House of Commons before Graham appointed him lieutenant colonel of the 1st North Carolina Infantry.

67. J. G. De Roulhac Hamilton, ed., *The Papers of Thomas Ruffin*, 4 vols. (Raleigh: Edwards & Broughton Printing Co., State Printers, 1918), vol. 2, p. 259.

68. *Carolina Watchman*, December 4, 1846, and January 29, February 5, February 19, February 26, March 5, 1847; *The Raleigh Star and North Carolina Gazette*, January 6, January 20, January 27, February, 3, and February 17, 1847; *North Carolina Standard*, January 27, February 10, 1847; House Ex. Doc. No. 78, pp. 230-31; *Hillsbourgh Recorder*, December 17, 1846, and February 4, 1847; Senate Ex. Doc. No. 62, pp. 50, 80, 87. For a discussion of the controversy surrounding Paine's appointment, see Wallace, "North Carolina in the War with Mexico," pp. 49-57.

69. *North Carolina Standard*, February 10, 1847.

70. Hamilton, ed., *The Papers of William A. Graham*, vol. 3, p. 216; Branham, *Register of Graduates.*, p. 120. Montfort Sidney Stokes was the son of the North Carolina governor and senator, Montfort Stokes. Although one source contends that he was an officer in the U.S. Navy (1829-1839), records at West Point reveal that he entered the U.S.M.A. in 1831 but failed to graduate. Stokes was the only one of the three field officers who was a Democrat. He was killed in the Civil War while leading a regiment of North Carolina volunteers at the Battle of Mechanicsville, Virginia, on June 26, 1862.

71. *Carolina Watchman*, October 14, 1847; *North Carolina Standard*, Raleigh, North Carolina, January 6, February 17, February 20, 1847; Hoffman, *North Carolina in the Mexican War*, pp. 16-17; Herbert Dale Pegg, *The Whig Party in North Carolina* (Chapel Hill: Colonial Press, Inc., 1969), pp. 144-47; J. G. De Roulhac Hamilton, *Party Politics in North Carolina, 1835-1860* (Durham: Seeman Printery, 1916), pp. 110-13; Clarence Clifford Norton, *The Democratic Party in Antebellum North Carolina, 1835-1861* (Chapel Hill: University of North Carolina Press, 1930), pp. 112-13, 154; Wallace, "Raising a Volunteer Regiment for Mexico, 1846-1847," pp. 28-31; Senate Ex. Doc. No. 62, pp. 49-50; Heitman, *Historical Register*, vol. 1, p. 1048; Quaife, ed., *Diary of James K. Polk*, vol. 3, p. 152. Louis D. Wilson (?-1847) was a popular North Carolina politician who was well known to Polk. Appointed colonel of the 12th U.S. Infantry, one the temporary regiments authorized by the Ten Regiment Bill, he died at Vera Cruz of yellow fever. When news of his death reached the president, Polk wrote, "He was a patriotic & highly intelligent man, and my personal friend. . . . I had a full and free confidential conversation with him on the subject of the War & the operations of the army in Mexico, & gave him my views fully."

72. Wallace, "North Carolina in the War with Mexico," p. 52.

73. *North Carolina Standard*, February 10, 1847.

74. Ibid., February 24, 1847.

75. Senate Ex. Doc. No. 62, p. 206.

76. *Hillsbourgh Recorder*, February 4, 1847. William H. Polk, the president's brother, was a major in the 3rd U.S. Dragoons.

77. Senate Ex. Doc. No. 62, p. 50.

78. Ibid., p. 206.

79. *Charlotte Daily Observer*, January 6, 1902.

80. Senate Ex. Doc. No. 62, p. 80.

81. Ibid., p. 69.

82. Ibid., p. 80.

83. Ibid., p. 208.

5.
The War Between the United States and Mexico

Miguel A. González Quiroga

It is said that wars usually begin many years before the first shot is fired. I believe this to be so, especially in the case of the war between the United States and Mexico. But how far back do we go? Ten years to the separation of Texas? Twenty-five years to the founding of the Mexican state? I would agree with those who hold that the die was cast when the United States was born as a nation and began its slow but inexorable expansion to the west.

The westward movement is one of several factors attributed to the war. You've heard them all: the slave interests of the South, the commercial interests of the Northeast, the land hunger of the West, Manifest Destiny, the warhawks, James K. Polk. For those who blame Mexico: her internal divisions, her inability to colonize and govern the northern lands, her rampant militarism, her unbounded arrogance.[1]

U.S. expansion, or growth, to use a less belligerent term, was, in my estimation, the principal cause of this great conflict. Without it, the war is simply incomprehensible. We could almost say that expansion—to borrow a phrase from William James—was an "irreducible brute fact."

Within the overall concept of expansionism stands the doctrine of Manifest Destiny which has an immense fascination for many scholars in Mexico. I wish to include in my essay a few words on the concept of Manifest Destiny. A second element of my analysis concerns the war in my home state of Nuevo León and a third involves the human element in this conflict, the impact that it had on people's lives, a topic which has been little explored.

Manifest Destiny

It is dangerous to underestimate the power of an idea, especially one that captures the imagination of a people. Manifest Destiny was such a concept. To extend U.S. democracy to the rest of the continent, was to place a mantle of legitimacy on what was essentially an insatiable ambition for land. Some have argued that it was villainy, to use an expression by Walter Lippman, clad in the armor of a righteous cause. It is difficult to argue against democracy and its extension to the farthest reaches of the continent although Josefina Zoraida Vázquez has pointed out that, at least in this case, extending the area of freedom also signified extending the area of slavery.[2]

The assertion of the superiority of the American race and the concomitant denigration of Mexico is another element of Manifest Destiny. It was Walt Whitman who stated: "what has miserable, inefficient Mexico—with her superstition, her burlesque upon freedom, her actual tyranny by the few over the many—what has she to do with the great mission of peopling the new world with a noble race? Be it ours, to achieve that mission!"[3]

Those of us who admire Whitman as the greatest of North American poets cannot but be disappointed at his stand on the war. Can this be the same poet who glorified equality and the respect for others when he said that "every atom belonging to me as good belongs to you?" Or when he wrote: "whoever degrades another degrades me, and whatever is done or said returns again to me?"[4]

How can we reconcile this contradiction? The poet of the body and of the soul himself explained it when he wrote: "I am vast, I contain multitudes."

It is a painful exercise to look in the mirror of our past and discover that we are found wanting. It is sobering to read that we were beaten because we were a backward and decaying people. I cannot think that Mariano Otero and Carlos María Bustamante, two of our illustrious ancestors, were the products of a decayed race. But we in Mexico cannot and do not ignore the weakness and the underdevelopment that was our lot in the early nineteenth century. Nor do we ignore that that underdevelopment was also the product of long and complex historical forces.

Manifest Destiny was a graceful way to justify something unjustifiable. It has not escaped our attention that Ulysses S. Grant, one of the most prominent American military men, and himself a participant in the war, wrote in his memoirs: "I do not think there ever was a more wicked war than that waged by the United States in Mexico. I thought so at the time, when I was a youngster, only I had not moral courage enough to resign."[5]

But as a historian I do not wish to judge or censure. Let me state my own views: expansion was a historical process that like a westward wind swept all before it. Not Mexico, not any force on this continent or any continent could have prevented it. This is not so much a question of good or evil, nor of guilt or innocence. It is more a question of demographics. European immigration led to an explosive growth of the population of the United States and this inevitably led to expansion. Expansion led to war.

On a more abstract level, we can equally admire U.S. democratic institutions and deplore the racism and feelings of superiority of some of her citizens.

War in Nuevo León

Beyond the causes and explanations of the conflict, Mexican historians have recently begun to explore the effects of the war on the regions and peoples who, directly or indirectly, suffered from its impact.

In many ways my home state of Nuevo León is a microcosm of the war. Prior to the conflict, Nuevo León had been an island of tranquility in a nation beset by anarchy and turmoil. This began to change after December 1845. Two military coups against the central government, one engineered by Mariano Paredes during that month and the other by Valentín Gómez Farías in August, 1846, hurled Nuevo León into the national storm.

Against the will of the *norteños*, Paredes and Gómez Farías imposed political and military rulers who caused dissension and division at a time that called for cohesion and strength. In the five-month period before the attack on Monterrey there were four different commanders of the northern army. And Manuel Maria de Llano, one of Nuevo León's most respected governors, wrote to Gómez Farías that none of these military leaders shared information or strategy with their successors.[6] On the political front there were even more stunning changes: four governors in one month before the battle. One can hardly expect to wage war under these circumstances.

The documents of the time also illustrate that there was a severe lack of arms, transportation and training for the local militias. Convincing the people to join the militia and fight the invader was another challenge.[7] This discovery was made by Santiago Vidaurri, who served in the state government many years before he became the strongman of the north. As general secretary of the state, Vidaurri authorized the menfolk to evacuate their families to the surrounding towns when it became known that Monterrey would be attacked. It was understood that the men would return to help defend the city. Many of them didn't, and Vidaurri reproached them with a warning of severe punishment if they failed to return.[8]

From these and other testimonials, it seems clear that many among the civilian population were not psychologically prepared for the conflict. The idea of fighting for the nation was not deeply rooted in the common people who had only a regional identification and no clear concept of nationalism. Mariano Otero, a prominent intellectual, stated that this was a problem that effected the entire country and in the case of Nuevo León, his observation appears to be true. In the political and military chaos, in the lack of preparedness, in the absence of an aggressive nationalism, Nuevo León was a faithful mirror of the nation.

One fact that is not often remembered is that Zachary Taylor's army arrived at Monterrey at a very inopportune moment. The city was about to celebrate its 250th anniversary on the 20th of September, 1846. All sorts of festivities had been planned. This was to be a moment of joy, jubilation, celebration. Instead the city was

A lithograph of "*Monterey, as seen from a house top . . . 1846*" by D. P. Whiting in *Army Portfolio, No. 1*, New York: G. & W. Endicott, 1846. (Mexican War Graphics Collection, Special Collections Division, The University of Texas at Arlington Libraries, Arlington, Texas.)

subjected to a furious onslaught unlike any it has witnessed before or since. The fighting left devastation and ruin that converted the town, in the words of one eyewitness, into a vast cemetery.[9]

Curiously, it was the civilian governor, Francisco de Paula y Morales, who urged the continuation of the battle while Pedro de Ampudia, the military chief, counseled surrender. Morales would never forgive him for this. He wrote to the federal authorities of the incompetence and cowardice shown by Ampudia during the fight for Monterrey.[10] Ampudia's actions eight years later when he was governor of Nuevo León lend credence to this interpretation. He ordered the confiscation and burning of all copies of a book which was highly critical of his actions during the siege of Monterrey.[11]

Taylor's army took control of the city on September 24th and stayed for almost two years until June, 1848, perhaps the longest occupation of any Mexican city during the war.

The two-year period has never been studied in depth but from what little is known about it, we may surmise that for many families it was the worst of times. Many civilians abandoned their homes, which were occupied by the invaders; many families fled to the interior. Those who stayed suffered at the hands of the ferocious volunteers, who went on a killing rampage in the early days of the occupation.[12]

Even some of Taylor's officers were horrified by the senseless killings. Ulysses S. Grant wrote to his wife: "some of the volunteers... seem to think it perfectly right to impose upon the people of a conquered city to any extent, and even to murder them where the act can be covered by the dark."[13]

The nightmare of the occupation is only part of the story. Not everyone suffered from the U.S. presence. Three towns in the path of the invaders suffered extensive damage and many haciendas and ranches were razed. But there is evidence which suggests that most of the towns were spared and that some of them even prospered by selling grain and livestock to the U.S. Army. This is only one of several paradoxes of this complex occupation.[14]

Another refers to the guerrilla bands which were mobilized to harass Taylor's army. An abundance of documents reveal that these irregular forces did more harm to the civilian population. We have read about Antonio Canales and the damage that he inflicted upon the invaders. But there is another story which until now has been largely hidden. Some of these guerrillas were thieves and freebooters, more interested in stealing from civilians than in combating the well armed convoys of the army of occupation.[15]

These guerrilla forces, at least in Nuevo León, were beyond the effective control of a state government, which tried but failed to maintain authority and all but disappeared during the critical year of 1847. Governor Morales had left Monterrey shortly after the battle and later established his government in Linares. But the nature of the occupation made it clear that he could not govern and he resigned in March, 1847. In this political vacuum the *municipios* of Nuevo León were left to fend for themselves and some discovered that they could, in fact, survive on their own. In a nation dominated by political centralism this perhaps was the first and only time that the *municipios* became momentarily free.

The Human Element in the War

After looking at dusty records, I try to imagine myself in the place of some of the people who were touched by the conflict. I'm particularly struck by farmers and farm laborers. Mexico was a rural country, the vast majority were rural folk far removed from newspapers or book learning. Their world view was necessarily limited: the seasons, the planting, the harvest, the weather. What could the loss of Texas possibly mean to them? Where was Texas anyway?

Although these rural people left no records, their attitudes somehow come through to us in the way their actions were described by government officials who tried to persuade them to take up arms against the invaders. Some went obediently, a few went patriotically, but many preferred to stay in their fields and work as if to say, "What has this got to do with me anyway?"

I have looked at several documents which appear to reveal this outlook. One of them is a letter from Manuel Flores, the alcalde of Salinas Victoria, who was called on to send eighty men to help defend

Pedro de Ampudia, 1850. (Mexican War Graphics Collection, Special Collections Division, The University of Texas at Arlington Libraries, Arlington, Texas.)

Monterrey. He wrote back saying that he could only recruit thirty-three. And he offered an eloquent testimony of what would occur if he forced the men to march to Monterrey:

The families will be exposed to murderous Indian raids.

The fields, planted with grains and beans, will be left unattended and the families reduced to indigence because it is well known that these farmers are exceedingly poor and their only means of subsistence derives from continuous and strenuous work.[16]

Did these men ignore the call to arms because they lacked courage or had a fear of dying? No. They faced death and danger all the time in the form of Indian attacks or deadly epidemics that wiped out whole families during such troubled times. So it is not for want of courage, it is something else: probably an ambivalence about the war combined with a pressing need to go about their work and continue to provide for their families. That was what mattered most to them.

Many years ago I saw a movie about a nuclear holocaust, *One Day After*. There is one scene that is seared into my memory. It is of a Kansas woman who is busy tending the beds and doing the housework even as the missiles are in the air and everyone is fleeing to underground shelters. She refuses to believe what was actually happening. I thought about this woman in connection with these Nuevo León farm people. They too refused to believe they were at war. They had too much to do. They couldn't be bothered or taken away from tasks which were life-giving and absolutely essential.

Behind the statistics and the descriptions of the carnage at battles like Buena Vista or Molino del Rey, there are the lives of countless families which were touched by the conflict. Little is known about this in Mexico owing to the dearth of written records. In the United States we have the accounts of some of the participants whose correspondence or diaries have survived and have been published. But what of the families, those who received a knock on their door by a stranger in uniform, informing them that their young man would never come home again?

This is surely what must have occurred to Mattie Hopkins, whose brave husband, Philip Barbour, died in the battle of Monterrey. On September 20th he had written in his journal that he was calm before the great battle. He was serene in the knowledge that in war a soldier's life becomes the property of his country and can only be preserved or taken from him by the will of God. God's will was made known on the following day. And upon his dying body and that of thousands of other young Americans was forged a mighty empire. But the sadness and suffering of the family remains. And who would dare say that the pain of this American family was any less than that of thousands of families in Mexico.[17]

As a young boy I read about the Monument to the Unknown Soldier, and I was fascinated by the concept. The very phrase has an aura of mystery about it. Surely, it is a monument to heroism, but in the absence of a grieving family it is something more. It is also a symbol created by a thankful nation which knows how to honor its dead and has refused to allow the world to forget. This soldier does not have to be known to be remembered because what he did and what he stood for is ultimately more meaningful than who he was.

I was reminded of this while reading some of the accounts of the Battle of Monterrey. Several U.S. soldiers observed a young maiden whose identity is still unknown. Under a rain of gunfire she ministered to the wounded and dying of both armies giving them water and tending their wounds. Seemingly oblivious to the murderous gunfire, she continued her valiant task and when she finished she began to leave the battlefield when suddenly she was struck by a bullet. She moved in agony for a short time, and then she lay still.[18] She was hastily buried the following day by the same soldiers who had witnessed her astonishing deed. Upon reading a passage like this, one stops to meditate: This is a woman, this is the stuff of which life is made and all else that happened in this great battle pales before it. There can be no greater moment, nor more sublime, for what can be greater than the self-sacrifice which gives life meaning and gives it worth? What can be more powerful than this lonely act of human courage?

Upon knowing of the valor of this unknown heroine the loss and the humiliation suffered in this terrible war begins to recede in the distance and we begin to realize that our strength comes not from the quantity or power of our guns but from the generosity and dignity of our people exemplified by this extraordinary woman.

In viewing the war from this perspective—far removed from geopolitical concerns—we get a different feeling about what was gained and what was lost. It has been said that the United States got land and Mexico got lessons. But the sudden acquisition of land became a burden. We return again to Whitman. In his 1856 "Song of the Open Road," he wrote:

> "It is provided in the essence of things that from any fruition of success, no matter what, shall come forth something to make a greater struggle necessary."[19]

Can this be a premonition of the fast approaching Civil War?

And what of Mexico? Granted, she gained some valuable lessons, not the least of which was a growing sense of nationalism. But she did not rise like the Phoenix from the ashes of the conflict as did Germany and Japan in this century. Indeed she had not flown very high in the thirty-year period before the war. In some ways Mexico still awaits her rise.

And many among our people still lament the land that was lost. But a nation is not finally measured in the quantity of its land but in the quality of its people and in the strength of its institutions.

NOTES

1 Ramón Eduardo Ruiz, ed., *The Mexican War, Was it Manifest Destiny?* (New York: Holt, Rinehart and Winston, 1963).

2. Josefina Zoraida Vázquez, "Los Primeros Tropiezos," in *Historia de México*, vol. 3, 3rd ed. (México City: El Colegio de México, 1981), p. 810.

3. Walt Whitman, *Brooklyn Daily Eagle*, July 7, 1846.

4. Taken from "Song of Myself," *Leaves of Grass and Selected Prose*, John Kouwenhoven, ed. (New York: Random House, 1950), p. 87.

5. George Seldes, comp., *The Great Quotations* (New York: Simon and Schuster, 1967), p. 960.

6. M. M. DeLlano to Gómez Farías, August 21, 1846, Gómez Farías Collection, Benson Latin American Collection, University of Texas at Austin.

7. Nuevo León State Archives, Ramo Militar, Box 51 (1846); David Alberto Cossío, *Historia de Nuevo León*, vol. 6 (Monterrey: Editorial J. Cantú Leal, 1936).

8. Nuevo León State Archives, Ramo Militar, Box 51, September 20, 1846.

9. "José Sotero Noriego" entry in *Diccionario Universal de Historia y de Geografía*, Manual Orozco y Berra, ed. Appendix, vol. 2 (México City: Imp. José Maria Andrade y F. Escalante, 1856), p. 883.

10. Cossio, *Historia de Nuevo León*, pp. 282-83.

11. Circular, March 24, 1854, Wallet 17-94, Arredondo Collection, Benson Latin American Collection.

12. Among others, see Robert H. Ferrell, ed., *Monterrey is Ours! The Mexican War Letters of Lieutenant Dana, 1845-1847* (Lexington: The University of Kentucky, 1990), James M. McCaffrey, *Army of Manifest Destiny: The American Soldier in the Mexican War, 1846-1848* (New York: New York University Press, 1992) and John R. Kenly, *Memoirs of a Maryland Volunteer, War with Mexico, in the Years 1846-1848* (Philadelphia: J. B. Lippincott & Co., 1873).

13. McCaffrey, *Army of Manifest Destiny*, p. 123.

14. Miguel A. González Quiroga, "Nuevo León ante la invasión norteamericana," in Laura Herrera Serna, ed., *México en guerra 1846-1848* (México City: Instituto Nacional de Antropología e Historia, 1997), pp. 425-71.

15. Ibid.

16. Nuevo León State Archives, Ramo Militar, Box 51, September 6, 1846.

17. Rhonda van Bibber Tanner, ed., *Journals of the Late Brevet Major Philip Norbourn Barbour and His Wife Martha Isabella Hopkins Barbour Written During the War with Mexico-1846* (New York: G. P. Putnam's Sons, 1936). p. 104.

18. *Houston Telegraph and Texas Register*, January 4, 1847, p. 2.

19. Taken from "Song of the Open Road."

6.
Journalism and the U.S.-Mexican War

by Mitchel Roth

The war with Mexico introduced the modern war correspondent to the world of journalism.[1] To this day the first reporter remains a somewhat elusive figure. Although this person was probably male and from New Orleans, evidence remains sketchy because of the exigencies of newspaper reporting in the 1840s. Until recently the history of the war correspondent has been neglected in part by the impersonal nature of the enterprise.[2] By-lines were seldom used; instead reporters were occasionally recognizable by their infrequent use of initials or clever pseudonyms. But more often than not, dispatches were published anonymously.

While the war with Mexico produced the first identifiable war correspondents, sketch artists had long recorded the glories and horrors of the battlefield. With technological advances in printmaking and the advent of photography in 1839, news took on a greater immediacy, especially with the clarity provided by the photographic image. Eyewitness reports ranged from on-the-spot coverage to second-hand reports gleaned days or weeks later. Sketches from field artists were later translated by lithographers far from the battlefield, sometimes losing accuracy in the process.[3] It is unknown how many journalists covered the conflict with Mexico. One contemporary estimated, however, that of the

ten to fifteen thousand persons connected with the press [nation-

wide], comprising editors, reporters, printers, pressmen, and dev-
ils...probably a thousand or fifteen hundred joined the invading
army.... At every stopping place and every town they captured,
they started a newspaper, and at the present moment there are
nearly a dozen Anglo American newspapers printed and circulated in the enemy's country. These journals, though small in size
are well got up and display considerable talent and ability. They
cannot fail in working a great change in the minds of the people;
and in the event of its becoming necessary to permanently occupy the whole of Mexico, will exercise an important influence in
the preservation of order and quiet.[4]

This passage is important because it demonstrates that at the time
journalists recognized that war reporting had come into its own, with
the editor perspicaciously concluding that "the press is altogether a
new element in the prosecution of war, and the troops of America
have the honor of being the first to introduce it."[5]

War with Mexico was declared barely two years after the advent
of the telegraph. By September, 1846, over 1200 miles of telegraph
lines connected the great cities of the United States. This compared
to only 175 miles in Britain. However, the expense of transmitting
the news over immense distances was prohibitive for most papers. It
quickly became apparent that the demand for national news stimu-
lated by the war would continue unabated. The conflict with
Mexico showed the value of war news in generating circulation.
With the growth of the penny press[6] and improved communication
conditions, the newspaper field became an increasingly lucrative
endeavor.

Newspapers relied on the horse express as far back as the beginning of the nineteenth century. Prior to the war with Mexico, in order
to insure swift and dependable service from New Orleans, newspapers
such as the Baltimore *Sun* employed the full range of transportation
and communication possibilities, including telegraph, railroads,
steamboats, stagecoaches and "sixty blooded horses," which signified
the number of horses used to forward the news.[7] Although newspa-

pers heralded various pony express services, which they claimed delivered the news by an unbroken chain of horsemen from New Orleans, in reality horsemen were employed to cover only those stretches not traversed by rail or telegraphic service. Late in 1847, however, the Philadelphia *Public Ledger*, the New York *Herald*, and the Baltimore *Sun* banded together to share the costs of a pony express service from New Orleans. This accommodation between the news services contributed ultimately to the establishment of the first Associated Press service in May 1848.[8]

Government couriers and news messengers risked life and limb traversing bandit-infested wilderness while keeping a wary eye out for Mexican guerrillas. Upon reaching Point Isabel on the Gulf of Mexico, messengers travelled by steamer to such southern ports as New Orleans and Mobile, before making their way by railroad to the nearest telegraph outpost. The telegraph revolutionized news reporting and introduced the modern war correspondent to a burgeoning literate public, hungering for news of America's war with Mexico.

Reliance solely on telegraph services for news-gathering left little room for error. Often rendered inoperable due to weather-related problems, it turned out that human nature was sometimes more truculent than Mother Nature. Tampering with telegraph lines became so endemic that in 1846 the Massachusetts legislature passed a law that prescribed a penalty of up to five years imprisonment and a $500 fine for "Any person who shall willfully and maliciously" interfere with the "Electro Magnetic Telegraph."[9] Other states soon followed suit.

With the outbreak of hostilities, New Orleans became the chief source of news concerning the conflict. Strategically situated, the New Orleans press played an integral role in the transmission of war news to the states. With virtually no direct newspaper coverage emanating from the Mexican side of the conflict, New Orleans rapidly established itself as both the army's chief news center and base of supplies. Due to its proximity to Mexico and Texas, New Orleans had devoted considerable attention to developments south of the border prior to the start of the fighting. According to one source, "Nowhere in America was the Mexican War more popular, and nowhere was the direct profit from that adventure in imperialism greater."[10]

The newspapers of New Orleans were at the forefront of battle reportage during the birth of this most dangerous profession.[11] These papers received much of the credit, since it was upon their reports that all other United States newspapers chiefly relied for war news. Most accounts of the U.S.-Mexican War were picked up from any of a dozen New Orleans newspapers, including the *Picayune*, the *Delta*, the *Crescent City*, the *Tropic* and the *Bee*.

Among the innovations in newspaper publication during this era was an increasing use of headlines. In a day when headlines were almost unknown, and when even the most cataclysmic news was set in five- or six-point type, ten-point headlines, such as those heralding the battles of Monterrey and Mexico City, must have made the event seem of monumental importance to its readers. Newspapermen were not only among the first to arrive in Mexico but also served early on as fighting men as well. The abundance of reporters in the field was at least partly due to the fact that so many newspapermen had volunteered to fight the Mexican army. At least twenty New Orleans printers could be found within the ranks of a single company of volunteers.[12] Among them were several correspondents of the New Orleans *Delta*, including James Freaner, who became one of George Wilkins Kendall's strongest competitors for war news gathering.

Other *Delta* war correspondents included George H. Tobin, whose vignettes were printed under "From Captain Tobin's Knapsack," and John H. Peoples who used the pseudonym "Chaparral." They were soon joined by the well-known southwestern humorist Thomas Bangs Thorpe, who after purchasing a share of the New Orleans *Tropic*, left to report south of the Río Grande.

The most celebrated and best-known correspondent was George Wilkins Kendall. Contrary to the status accorded him as being the first war correspondent, there were probably other representatives of New Orleans' nine newspapers who could have claimed a similar distinction.[13] Born in Mount Vernon, New Hampshire, in 1809, Kendall gained experience first as a printer in Vermont and on Horace

George Wilkins Kendall about 1849, prominent war correspondent and publisher. (Kendall Family papers, Special Collections Division, The University of Texas at Arlington Libraries, Arlington, Texas.)

Greeley's *New-Yorker*, before relocating to New Orleans where he co-founded with Francis Lumsden the first inexpensive daily newspaper in the city, the *Picayune*, in 1837.[14]

Soon after war broke out along the Río Grande, Kendall attached himself to General Zachary Taylor's command.[15] Thirsting to see the battle front first-hand he joined the Texas Rangers under Captain Ben McCulloch. Although he missed the early battles of 1846 at Palo Alto and Resaca de la Palma, his reputation soared as he covered most of the battles of Generals Taylor and Winfield Scott, taking a bullet in the leg in the process at Chapultepec. At the fall of Monterrey he even captured a Mexican flag, which he sent home to his paper as a trophy.

Kendall organized his own pony express in Mexico, which doubled as a courier service for official dispatches. Demonstrating the importance placed on his "postal" service by soldiers far from home was an April 19, 1847, letter from Ralph W. Kirkham in Vera Cruz to his wife, in which he commented "We got the news this evening, just before I left town, by Kendall's Express which is ahead of the government one, that General Scott met Santa Anna at the pass of Cerro Gordo, and succeeded in obtaining a victory."[16]

New Orleans journalists like Freaner and Kendall organized swift courier services for their papers, but more than one of their messengers was waylaid, found hanged by the neck with the warning note "Correo de los Yanquis" pinned to his clothing. Kendall's system of delivering war news provided a model for others providing similar services. His fleet of couriers, with the help of steamers, became known as "Mr. Kendall's express." One report has Kendall chartering a steamer to deliver a dispatch from Vera Cruz to New Orleans at the cost of $5,000. The *Picayune*, under the aegis of Kendall became a model of efficiency, with fast sloops actually carrying printers and their type cases to meet the slower steamers from Vera Cruz with the news, insuring that by the time the printers debarked at the Crescent City the dispatches were already set in type and ready for press.

Kendall witnessed such events as the capture of the San Patricio flag at the strategic battle of Churubusco, the carnage at Cerro Gordo, and many incidents of equal importance. At Churubusco, he

VOLUME IX.]   NEW ORLEANS, MONDAY MORNING, JANUARY 4, 1847.   [NUMBER 47.

The masthead of the New Orleans *Picayune*—a newspaper that actively supported and reported on the U.S.-Mexican War. (Special Collections Division, The University of Texas at Arlington Libraries, Arlington, Texas.)

was present for one of the most controversial episodes of the war when the seventy-two members of the captured San Patricio battalion were accused of desertion, a capital offense. Kendall was not the lone witness from the press corps. Editors from the *American Star*, which provided the U.S. Army with news services, reported the whipping and branding accorded those prisoners not sentenced to be executed. However, most of the U.S. servicemen and many representatives of the press felt that the punishment was not unduly harsh due to wartime circumstances. William C. Tobey, editor and publisher of the *North American* in Mexico City during its occupation, noted that "We can paint no man, however cursed by conscience and despised by all...so infamously degraded as the traitor.... There is no punishment too severe for the traitor; no infamy too blackening for his name."[17]

Kendall's dispatches in the *Picayune* offer insight into the tribulations faced by reporters during the war. While covering the battle of Cerro Gordo on April 17, 1847, Kendall recounted, "I write this in great haste, and with noise, confusion and everything else around me. You cannot appreciate the victory.... No time to say another word. I send this off by an express."[18] Two days later he reported "I write this amid confusion of all kinds, and with no other table than knees.... A hundred Mexican officers are around me, making out their paroles, while our dead are being carried by and consigned to their long resting-place by the road."[19]

Kendall's partner, the North Carolinian Frances Lumsden, later joined him in Mexico. At the outbreak of the war, Lumsden began organizing volunteers into the Orleans regiment. However, when a better equipped company from Georgia known as the Gaines Rangers elected Lumsden as their captain, he ended his recruitment drive and left for the border with the Rangers. Perhaps he should have stuck to his original plan, for after reaching the Mexican border came word that the ship carrying their supplies and ammunition had gone down in a storm. The ill-fated Georgian regiment disbanded in Matamoros shortly after the enlistment period ended. Lumsden eventually hooked up with the *Picayune* staff and covered General Scott's Vera

Cruz campaign in early 1847 while attached as an aide to the staff of a General Shields. In March 1847 his days in the field were numbered after fracturing his leg in a fall from his horse. It seemed that anything Lumsden contrived to do involving sea transport was doomed to disaster as evidenced by his interlude with the Gaines Rangers. His bad luck came to an end in September, 1860, when Lumsden and his family perished with 300 passengers when the steamer *Lady Elgin* sank in a storm on Lake Michigan after a collision with another boat.[20]

Next to Kendall, perhaps the most important correspondent for the *Picayune* was Christopher Mason Haile, a protégé of Kendall's and the first member of his growing staff. He attended West Point briefly in the late 1830s before resigning his appointment and moving to Louisiana where he joined the staff of the *Planter's Gazette*. He later quit the paper for the *Picayune* and developed a following for his whimsical pieces under the byline of "Pardon Jones."

Haile's legacy as a war correspondent was given early prominence due to his courageous and exhaustive coverage of the Battle of Monterrey in September, 1846. In October, the *Picayune* published several letters from one soldier who witnessed Haile's part in the action reporting that he "saw Haile several times during the fight riding about quite indifferent to the balls which fell around him. Although he did not run into danger, he did not appear to try to avoid it when it visited him."[21]

It typically took days for correspondents to sort out the complexities of protracted battles that often took place over a wide area. Haile reported his technique for covering the battle of Monterrey:

> By riding over the ground with officers who participated in those sanguinary engagements, by many inquiries, and frequently referring to the reports and private journals of officers, as well as to the official maps, and by carefully noting down the information thus obtained, I feel confident that I can now give as correct an account of the operations of the divisions of Gen. Twiggs and Gen. Butler as will be published before the appearance of the regular reports.

Although Haile has been criticized for reporting the battle as if he witnessed the entire affair, he never claimed that he did. He explained immediately after the fighting that he could only offer information piece-meal and anecdotally since he could "only speak of the general operations on the east of the town."[22]

Clearly Haile was one of the best-known journalists in the field. In an early history of the war, Abiel Abbot Livermore made reference to "the army correspondent of the *New Orleans Picayune*, Mr. Haile." In a later work detailing the contributions of the Texas Rangers to the American war effort, Samuel C. Reid noted that "In order to give to the reader all of the ingredients of the campaign...we shall give the letters of Mr. Haile, or made extracts from them, relating to the army where we were not in person."[23]

Following the victory at Monterrey, Kendall left for New Orleans, while Haile remained with Taylor's forces. Haile compiled a list of the dead and wounded and wrote an informative account of the aftermath listing captured weapons and munitions as well as names, ranks, places and dates for the casualties, both dead and wounded. When Haile left the front, his editors hoped it would be "temporary." His paper reported that he was held in such high esteem by General Worth, who noted "Should hostilities be resumed...I hope you will return to the army, and with a command, for which your military education and recent experience particularly fit you."[24]

After Monterrey, Haile returned to the lighter fare for which he was best known, writing satirical sketches in the form of reports from the quixotic "Pardon Jones" to General Taylor and President Polk. Before returning to New Orleans for good, Haile was assigned to cover the Vera Cruz campaign, where his West Point training was put to good use when he was commissioned as a lieutenant, although "it was hoped by his friends that his military education and experience would command him to a higher grade of service."[25]

Lending credence to the primitive nature of reporting in this era, particularly in a foreign country, was the problem of Spanish translations. Names and places were often obfuscated because of differences in spelling and interpretation. Even the *Daily Picayune* admitted that the name of one town, Cerralvo or Serralvo, "has been spelled differently in our columns—Mr. Kendall preferring the former and Mr. Haile the latter mode, and each giving a fanciful etymology of the word."[26]

A high premium was placed on anyone fluent in Spanish, especially when it came to translating correspondence from General Santa Anna to Zachary Taylor on a regular basis. In one instance a topographical engineer translated Santa Anna's account of the battle of Buena Vista from the Mexico City *El Republicano* for the *Picayune*, which pronounced it "One of the most extraordinary documents I ever met."[27] In another instance a week had passed without any information on the situation of the army of the Río Grande, and the *Picayune* was forced to derive its information from a letter from Santa Anna to the U.S. War Department.[28]

With at least fifty Mexican newspapers covering the war, accounts gleaned from the enemy press allowed Americans to peruse the Mexican point of view. Propaganda was a two-edged sword and could be used to rally patriotic support or whip the opponent into a frenzy. In one "hasty translation" a column from the *La Columna de la Libertad* described the Mexican army as "better disciplined, more inured to hardships...the chances of war are in our favor. Let the Americans suffer any reverse...and their ruin will be complete."[29]

One of Kendall's chief rivals was James L. Freaner, correspondent for the New Orleans *Delta*, who published his war dispatches under the pseudonym "Mustang." Although he reportedly acquired his sobriquet at the battle of Monterrey when he supposedly killed an officer of the lancers in hand-to-hand combat and seized his charger, Freaner was actually writing under this moniker as early as June 1846, several months before the September battle.[30] Twice he was chosen to relay official dispatches From General Scott to Washington in November, 1847. After the cessation of hostilities in February, 1848, Nicholas Trist delegated him to carry the Treaty of Guadalupe Hidalgo to Washington.[31]

Freaner's reputation as an intrepid member of the press was well founded. On one occasion toward the end of the war, he arrived in Puebla bearing dispatches from General Winfield Scott after a fourteen-hour horseback ride from Mexico City. Two hours later Freaner left for Vera Cruz, which he hoped to reach that night. The *Flag of Freedom* described his peregrinations as "what one might call quick travelling," and deduced that "his despatches must be of a highly important character to require such great haste." Contrary to typical accounts that paint these excursions as solitary treks, on this mission Freaner was accompanied by a three-man escort. Freaner's prestige was apparently widespread by the end of the conflict, as evidenced by several blurbs in the Puebla, Mexico, *Flag of Freedom* which described him as "the well known and truly celebrated correspondent 'Mustang,' of the New Orleans *Delta*."[32]

War reporters served the army in other capacities as well. Besides their customary duties, they delivered letters back to the states for soldiers. Lieutenant Napoleon Jackson Tecumseh Dana, serving with General Zachary Taylor's army between 1845 and 1847, reported in his diary that he wrote a letter to his wife and "gave it to a reporter of the [New Orleans] *Picayune* who is along, for if there happened to be a chance of getting a letter off, he would be sure to find it out in order to send his reports."[33]

Compared to war coverage in the twentieth century, there seemed to be few constraints placed on the press in Mexico. Many letters by members of the U.S. Army printed in the *Picayune*, were published pseudononomously, however. It is difficult to say, for instance, whether "Paisano" was worried about repercussions from his reports, or whether there was some type of unwritten prohibition about discussing certain aspects of the war. What is clear is that some letters were published that can be construed as anti-war in nature. According to one letter written by a member of the commissary department at Buena Vista to his father: "I went over the battle-field after the fight, and of all the shocking, and most horrible sights I ever witnesses, this exceeded. Hundreds of dead, wounded, dying—some with their heads, arms, legs off, and some torn literally to pieces by shell and shot."[34] This description, like many others, contrasts markedly with future war reportage that took care to soften the descriptions of war in order to maintain support at home.

Newspapers outside the deep South tended not to send corre-spondents to cover the war, although there were some in evidence. While most Missouri papers reprinted accounts of the U.S.-Mexican War from New Orleans papers, as did newspapers in the East, news-papers such as the Jefferson *Inquirer* were represented along the Río Grande. From mid-1846 through the end of the war, Lucian J. Eastin, an officer among the Missouri volunteers as well as a staff member of the capital city *Inquirer*, sent back interesting, often laconic copy: "During the day we encountered a ferocious enemy in the form of gnats ... travelled 18 miles and reached the Little Arkansas; suffered much from want for water; frequently drank out of wagon ruts." Eastin's stories, published under the initial "E," ran the gamut from ordinary tales of camp life to brief reports of skirmishes with the enemy, including one which described "our loss, one killed, one mor-tally wounded, and seven so wounded as to recover without any loss of limbs."[35]

Although the best-known correspondents represented the New Orleans press, other less celebrated reporters have emerged as worthy exemplars of the tradition. According to historian Nicholas Joost, Richard Smith Elliott, a Missouri volunteer and regular correspon-dent for the St. Louis *Reveille*, "has a good claim to be considered— along with the famous George W. Kendall of the New Orleans *Picayune*—as one of the earliest American war correspondents."[36] Elliott accompanied General Stephen Watts Kearny's Army of the West to Santa Fe and was best known for his pieces signed with his moniker "John Brown."[37]

In September 1846 the New York *Herald* claimed five reporters in Mexico, "boasting that the group had more talent than those of any other paper."[38] And in the following May the *Herald* announced its intention to describe the leading stories "as daguerreotype reports— written accounts with the accuracy and immediacy of a photographic view."[39] Other papers followed the *Herald*'s lead, including the New York *Sun*, which published the dispatches of Jane McManus Storms, the only known female correspondent to cover the war from the front lines.[40] A well-known, somewhat iconoclastic letter-writer in

Washington during the 1840s and '50s, Storms (or Storm) had met President Polk and prominent members of his cabinet. According to one account she had arrived in Mexico City on a clandestine wartime peace mission and in the process became the only correspondent to report from behind the Mexican lines.[41] Under the pseudonyms "Montgomery" and "Cora Montgomery" she had well established credentials by the time she filed her first battle report. Writing from the Mexican seaport of Vera Cruz on January 13, 1847, Storms predicted that the city would resist the U.S. invasion and in the process "prove themselves better soldiers than the regular army...for they are animated by a proud, inflexible Spanish resentment against their invaders."[42] In another dispatch she noted that "The deplorable inefficiency of the navy has added at least a year to the...war." Storms continued to unleash a withering barrage of criticism at the ineptitude of the navy, writing: "U.S. Commodore David E. Conner could easily have taken the city seven months earlier, before the scurvy decimated his men."[43] Despite her penchant for scathing invective, Storms was held in such good stead with U.S. authorities that she was chosen to tackle the hazardous journey to Vera Cruz, some 200 miles away to inform General Scott of events taking place in Mexico City.

Jane McManus Storms was one of the few writers to criticize U.S. military efforts as well as the actions of her fellow reporters. Like Storms, Christopher Haile of the *Picayune* unleashed a withering attack on mismanagement of the war, particularly the inept care of the sick and wounded. In November, 1846, he was aboard a ship ferrying casualties back to New Orleans, when he noticed unattended soldiers, including many who had lost arms and legs: "Will you believe me when I tell you that with all these sick and wounded and dying men, not a surgeon or nurse was sent along to attend them, not a particle of medicine furnished, not a patch of linen for dressing."[44]

While many reporters were sent from desk duty to the field, others had made arrangements before enlisting with their hometown newspapers to send home dispatches. Editors as well as their underlings served in the army, with sixteen from Massachusetts alone. During a voyage of several days Captain Robert Anderson, an artillery officer, established a friendship with another officer aboard ship. It was only upon landing at Vera Cruz that he learned that his friend Anderson was a regular correspondent for the New Orleans *Delta* and the Baltimore *Sun*. The reporter assured his new friend that "in his last letter to the *Delta*, he mentioned that I was well." Anderson wrote his wife:

> This information was most kindly meant for you, but he did not know where you were, or he would have had a copy sent to you. I am sorry that he mentioned my name at all as the custom of recording everybody's deeds has become so common, that it is almost more creditable not to be among the distinguished.[45]

Virtually every company of volunteers counted at least one printer within their ranks. There was little to distinguish the newspaperman from the printer in this era, hence "printer" became synonymous with reporter during the war with Mexico. Even typesetters, experienced with most functions of the newspaper business, were viewed as potential correspondents.

The establishment of various camp newspapers during the conflict was a new development in reporting, with nearly a score published by soldier-printers on small handpresses to serve the various army corps. Some efforts were amateurish, lasting only a few issues, while the more professional organs lasted for several months. During the war, an army newspaper could be found in virtually every camp. The most enduring of these was the *American Flag*, serving Taylor's army. It was first published at Matamoros and was used by many papers as a chief source of news from the front. Among the other army papers were *The American Star* at Jalapa, *The Eagle* at Vera Cruz and *The Picket Guard* at Saltillo.

Occupation newspapers, such as the appropriately named *Flag of Freedom* based in Puebla, made no attempt to hide their expansionist and racist sentiments: "Our mission to Mexico was prompted by no other motive than a wish to be instrumental in planting the 'Flag of Freedom' firmly in its soil, and to leave it there in the keeping of a regenerated nation." Storms criticized the biased journalism of these papers, noting that one of them was "too devoted to their army to be entirely just." Concerning this form of enterprise as a whole she noted, "Truth always goes home from the seat of war dressed exclusively in robes of American manufacture."[46]

There were numerous writers and printers who founded their own newspapers in Mexico's occupied cities, rather than simply report the news back to their bases of operation in the United States. These fledgling enterprises became known collectively as the "Anglo-Saxon press." Beginning with the Corpus Christi *Gazette*, they would eventually number twenty-five in fourteen cities. Most were ephemeral, although some lasted until the end of the conflict. The first English-language newspaper to be published in Mexico City was the *American Star*, founded during the occupation of the Mexican capital by two enterprising journalists from New Orleans, John H. Peoples and John R. Barnard. According to the *Picayune*, the *Star* staff "adopted the military maxim of foraging on the enemy as the types, presses, and materials of the *Star* were taken from the Mexican Jalapa newspaper."[47] One paper described the *Star* as the "pioneer of the American press in Mexico."[48] George Ballentine, an English soldier in the United States Army, reported that the newspaper was published once a week for six cents an issue. In his autobiography, published in 1854, Ballentine remembered the *American Star* as being "only purchased by the Army," therefore "its circulation must have been rather limited; but it usually contained a good many items of army intelligence, and a considerable number were brought home to friends in the States, both by officers and soldiers."[49]

Having already established the Vera Cruz *Eagle* and other papers, editors Peoples and Barnard set to work in Mexico City publishing proclamations and orders of U.S. military commanders as well as sundry news items. The real significance of these papers to the American public was that they offered more reliable news than releases coming by way of official and military channels. Evidently, not all readers were convinced of the credibility of the occupation periodicals. In a letter to his wife, Winslow F. Sanderson noted that they "will publish anything for money."[50] The fledgling occupation papers were under no illusion as to their position in the journalistic pecking order. In the spring of 1847, *The American Pioneer* of Monterrey noted that "it is to the New Orleans papers that the whole country looks for early and correct information, and their statements are generally copied and believed, no matter how erroneous."[51]

The majority of the "Anglo-Saxon Press" offered both an English and Spanish section in its pages. Most operated on a shoestring budget as evidenced by the Saltillo *Picket Guard*, which suffered from a shortage of the letter "w." The resourceful editors did not miss a beat however, and found that a double "v" worked just as well. A typical example can be found the May 10, 1847 issue which noted

> There has alvvays [sic] existed betvveen [sic] Gen. Taylor and Gen. Wood the most perfect confidence. There has been no difference in their vievvs [sic], and no one I am sure, vvill [sic] see the article in question vvith [sic] so much regret as Gen. Taylor.[52]

Among the more short-lived papers was the *Yankee Doodle*, which lasted for six issues in 1847. It was circulated out of the offices of the *North American* in Mexico City and was more a vehicle for humor than hard news. One competitor, the *Daily American Star*, noted the existence of the paper simply because of "the fact that the 'greaser' newsboys could not pronounce the title."[53] The *North American*, under the management of William C. Tobey, who wrote under the pseudonym "John of York," was remembered as presenting "a neat appearance, and is conducted with spirit and good taste."[54]

Newspapermen in Mexico often suffered dry spells when there was little newsworthy to print. To fill the gaps they resorted to publishing contributions from the ranks. While much of the soldiers' contributions ended up in the trash, some of the rejected material served as entertaining grist for the editor's columns. On January 22, 1848 a column appeared in the *North American* which noted that "Our ordnance friend is informed that his poem is the best we have seen of the kind, but not liking that particular kind, we decline publishing it." The following month saw the publication of a similar column announcing that "A.H.H. your rhymes are not readable; some of the words are nearly obliterated. The poem must have been written on the bottom of a camp kettle." Often editors were so hard pressed to find something to print they simply published passages directly out of books, as the *North American* did with the poems of Victor Hugo and the works of the historian William H. Prescott.

The occupation newspapers boosted the morale of soldiers, who had never travelled so far from home. The engineer, lawyer and West Point graduate, Colonel Samuel Ryan Curtis, made a habit of mining occupation newspapers for mention of his unit to send home to his family. He recorded in his diary that when he noticed an article referring to his unit's position in the *American Flag* on August 12, 1846, that "this is the first notice of us in a foreign press [and] I will attach the article." A month later he noted that

> The flag [*American Flag*] of today makes favourable mention of my regiment. These are hard earned but respected compliments. I do not know a man connected with the press here, and suppose therefore I must deserve some of it. I'll keep these little complements, they are the tracks we make in the sands of life; and these being far from friends and kindred they should be preserved.[55]

On April 21, 1847, Curtis reported that the previous week's Saltillo *Picket Guard* spoke "so favourable of my regiment I will here attach the paragraph so as to preserve it."[56]

Newspaper publishers in Mexico did not have a monopoly on ingenuity. Newsboys often sold papers for several times the regular price. Editors responded by printing the price on the front page. This did not deter the newsboys who simply folded the offending cost under and went on selling the papers at their chosen amount. Editors would often caution readers by printing warnings of the sordid practice. The *Picayune* was forced to publish a warning that "the news boys, in selling the paper, will on no account charge anything for the additional sheet," with the caveat that if any employees were reported they would be discharged.[57] Besides the enterprising newsboys, papers also lost revenue to vendors who saw an opportunity for profit by cutting newspapers that had both English and Spanish sections in half and selling each at full price.

During the first year of the war, coverage was disparaged and often lost its appeal to its readership due to the seeming inability of papers to print stories in a timely fashion. In one instance news concerning the battles of Buena Vista and Vera Cruz in February and March 1847, did not reach Boston until the last day of March and since it was published on April 1, most readers assumed it was an April Fool's joke when the stories appeared in *The Boston Journal*. The tardiness was finally addressed by several papers which banded together to gather war news. In many cases these newspaper consortiums would offer more dependable war coverage than the national government. This was exemplified on April 10, 1847, when President Polk and his cabinet were notified of the surrender of Vera Cruz by the *Sun* rather than through official channels.[58]

In many cases newspapers reached audiences late because of the ineptness of the postal service. The *Picayune* was forced to address the shortcomings of mail service with an editorial criticizing "the shameful management" of the mails, after a deluge of complaints reached the newspaper detailing the "non-reception of papers."[59]

While most Americans reveled in the outcome of the war with Mexico and avidly followed dispatches from south of the border, others had begun to weary of the saturation of war reporting. It is possible that the preponderance of reports glamorizing the carnage in Mexico prepared the nation for the bloodletting to come in the next decade at home. In 1850 the sagacious Unitarian minister and peace advocate, Abiel Abbot Livermore, lamented that

> One of the unhappy consequences of the war is, that it has thus created a literature adverse to morals, refinement and religion. This war literature has circulated through the newspapers and cheap works over the whole land. The lives of victorious generals, the bloody feats of prowess, the histories of battles and sieges, have formed a good part of the reading of the mass of the people, and especially of many young persons, during the past three years.... The natural effect upon society of such reading, and war-songs, and

exhibitions is exceedingly unfavorable to all the leading moral interests of a free country.[60]

Perhaps, Livermore recognized the fact that the constant barrage of war news inured the younger generation to violence, a generation that would make up so much of the fodder in the coming sectional conflict. The minister warned that "The seed of future wars has thus been sown broadcast over our country, and wrong impressions have been made upon thousands of young and ductile minds which will never be effaced."[61]

NOTES

1. This is a subject of much contention since firsthand war coverage has appeared in newsprint since the American Revolution. Isaiah Thomas's eyewitness account of the Battle of Concord appeared in the Worcester *Massachusetts Spy*, and in 1837 Charles Lewis Gruneison reported the Carlist War in Spain as a special correspondent for the London *Morning Post*. While prior to the war with Mexico, freelancers and letter writers not associated with any particular newspapers sent firsthand accounts to various publications, a distinction should be made here between the amateur unaffiliated journalist and the paid employee of newspapers sent to cover foreign wars. What elevated these reporters to the status of first modern war reporters was their access to the telegraph and the penny presses, which lent an air of immediacy to this developing enterprise.

2. For an in-depth survey on U.S.-Mexican War journalists see Thomas Reilly, "American Reporters and the Mexican War, 1846-1848," Ph.D. dissertation, University of Minnesota, 1984.

3. Martha A. Sandweiss, Rick Stewart, and Ben W. Huseman, *Eyewitness to War: Prints and Daguerreotypes of the Mexican War, 1846-1848* (Fort Worth: Amon Carter Museum, 1989); Ron Tyler, *The Mexican War: A Lithographic Record* (Austin: Texas State Historical Association, 1973).

4. *Flag of Freedom*, Feb. 19, 1848.

5. Ibid.

6. In the decades leading up to the war, newspapers were typically sold by subscription at about six cents per copy. With daily circulation averaging close to 1000, these papers catered to a more elite clientele. With technological advances

increasing printing capacity and the emergence of upwardly mobile workers and a middle class, publishers launched popular newspapers that were lower priced and were sold on the streets by vendors for one or two cents, hence the growth of the penny papers or "penny press."

7. Gerald Johnson, Frank R. Kent, H.L. Mencken and Hamilton Owens, *The Sunpapers of Baltimore, 1837-1937* (New York: Alfred A. Knopf, 1937), p. 74; J. Thomas Scharf, *History of Baltimore City and County* (Philadelphia: Louis H. Everts, 1881), p. 619. For an excellent history of this periodical, see Harold A. Williams, *The Baltimore Sun, 1837-1987* (Baltimore: Johns Hopkins Press, 1987).

8. Frank M. O'Brien, *The Story of the Sun, New York: 1833-1928* (New York: D. Appleton and Co., 1928), p. 113; Oliver Gramling, AP, *The Story of News* (Port Washington, New York: Kennikat Press, 1969), pp. 19-21.

9. *National Police Gazette*, vol. 2 (November 21, 1846), p. 11.

10. Harold Sinclair, *The Port of New Orleans* (Garden City, New York: Doubleday, Doran and Company, Inc., 1942), p. 195.

11. The best account of New Orleans newspapers during the Mexican War can be found in Tom Reilly, "The War Press of New Orleans: 1846-1848," *Journalism Quarterly*, vol. 13 (Autumn-Winter 1986), pp. 86-95.

12. Robert W. Johanssen, *To the Halls of the Montezumas* (New York: Oxford University Press, 1985), p. 17.

13. Fayette Copeland, *Kendall of the Picayune* (Norman: University of Oklahoma Press, 1943; reprint edition 1970). Based upon Kendall's unpublished manuscript of some 1000 pages, this is the only full-scale biography of the life and times of the man. It should be noted, however, that Kendall wrote his recollections almost twenty years after the war, lending it a perspective that blunts its value as a primary source for the Mexican War. John Hohenberg, *Foreign Correspondence* (New York: Columbia University Press, 1964), p. 40; Kendall's Mexican War reportage has been collected and published in Lawrence Delbert Cress, ed., *Dispatches from the Mexican War* (Norman: University of Oklahoma Press, 1999).

14. Its name was derived from a coin used during the time of the Spanish presence in the area which was worth about six cents, the price of the paper.

15. Kendall's exploits in the war were not his first in Mexico. In 1841 he participated in the ill-fated Texas expedition to Santa Fe, in which he was captured and imprisoned in Mexico City for several months. He chronicled his experiences in the bestselling *Narrative of the Texan Santa Fe Expedition*, published in 1844 (Chicago: R.R. Donnelly and Sons, Co., 1929).

16. *The Mexican Journal and Letters of Ralph W. Kirkham*, Robert Ryall Miller, ed. (College Station: Texas A&M University Press, 1991), p. 4.

17. Quoted in Robert Ryal Miller, *Shamrock and Sword: The Saint Patrick's Battalion in the U.S.-Mexican War* (Norman: University of Oklahoma Press, 1989), p. 109.

18. *Daily Picayune*, May 1, 1847. Hereafter cited as *Picayune*.

19. Ibid.

20. Copeland, *Kendall of the Picayune*, p. 155.

21. *Picayune*, October 22, 1846.

22. Ibid., November 4, 1846.

23. Abiel Abbot Livermore, *The War with Mexico Reviewed* (Boston: W. Crosby and H.P. Nichols, 1850), p. 141; Samuel C. Reid, *The Scouting Expeditions of McCulloch's Texas Rangers* (Philadelphia: J.W. Bradley, 1859), p. 121.

24. *Picayune*, November 19, 1846.

25. Ibid., April 10, 1847.

26. Ibid., October 30, 1846.

27. Ibid., April 9, 1847.

28. Ibid., March 21, 1847.

29. Ibid., December 11, 1846.

30. Thomas J. Farnham, "Nicholas Trist and James Freaner and the Mission to Mexico," *Arizona and the West*, vol. 2 (Autumn 1969), p. 254. For more on Freaner see William A. DePalo, Jr., "James L. Freaner," in *The United States and Mexico at War*, Donald S. Frazier, ed. (New York: Simon and Schuster, 1998), p. 165; Jimmy L. Bryan, Jr., "Correspondence of the U.S.-Mexican War (1846-1848) from the New Orleans *Delta*," unpublished manuscript, Center for Southwestern Studies and the History of Cartography, University of Texas at Arlington (n.d.). Bryan identifies the war correspondents for the *Delta*, and cites the dates of each contribution and location of correspondents during the conflict. According to Bryan's research, Freaner contributed 122 pieces to the newspaper during the conflict.

31. F. Lauriston Bullard, *Famous War Correspondents* (Boston: Little, Brown and Company, 1914), pp. 362-63.

32. *Flag of Freedom*, February 5, 1848.

33. Robert H. Ferrell, ed., *Monterrey is Ours! The Mexican War Letters of Lieutenant Dana, 1845-1847* (Lexington: University of Kentucky Press, 1990), p. 119.

34. *Picayune*, April 27, 1847.

35. Quoted in William H. Taft, *Missouri Newspapers* (Columbia: University of Missouri Press, 1964), p. 44.

36. Nicholas T. Joost, "Reveille in the West: Western Travelers in the St. Louis *Weekly Reveille*, 1844-50," in *Travelers on the Western Frontier*, John Francis McDermott, ed. (Urbana: University of Illinois Press, 1970), pp. 216-17.

37. *The Mexican War Correspondence of Richard Smith Elliott*, Mark L. Gardner and Marc Simmons, eds. (Norman: University of Oklahoma Press, 1997).

38. Johanssen, *To The Halls of the Montezumas*, p. 18.

39. Sandweiss, et al., *Eyewitness to War*, p. 18.

40. See Tom Reilly, "Jane McManus Storms: Letters From the Mexican War, 1846-1848," *Southwestern Historical Quarterly*, vol. 85 (July 1981), pp. 21-44; For more biographical information, see Walter Webb, H. Bailey Carroll and Eldon Stephen Branda, eds., *The Handbook of Texas*, 3 vols. (Austin 1952), vol. 2; and Edward T. James, ed., *Notable American Women, 1607-1950*, 3 vols. (Cambridge: Belknap Press of Harvard University Press, 1971), vol. 1, pp. 315-17.

41. Reilly, "Jane McManus Storms," p. 23.

42. Ibid., p. 31.

43. Ibid.

44. *Picayune*, November 14, 1846.

45. *An Artillery Officer of the Mexican War, 1846-7: Letters of Robert Anderson* (New York: G.P. Putnam's Sons, 1911), p. 77.

46. Quoted in Lota M. Spell, "The Anglo-Saxon Press in Mexico, 1846-1848," in *American Historical Review*, vol. 38 (October, 1932).

47. *Picayune*, May 9, 1847.

48. *Flag of Freedom*, November 10, 1847.

49. George Ballentine, *Autobiography of an English Soldier in the United States Army* (New York: Stringer & Townsend, 1854), p. 140.

50. Winslow F. Sanderson to his wife, May 7, 1847, Winslow F. Sanderson Collection, Rice University, Houston, Texas.

51. *American Pioneer*, May 18, 1847.

52. Saltillo *Picket Guard*, May 10, 1847, Natchez Trace Collection, Center for American History, University of Texas, Austin.

53. *Daily American Star*, October 10, 1847.

54. *Flag of Freedom*, November 10, 1847.

55. Joseph E. Chance, ed., *Mexico Under Fire: Being the Diary of Samuel Ryan Curtis, 3rd Ohio Volunteers Regiment, During the American Military Occupation of Northern Mexico, 1846-1847* (Fort Worth: Texas Christian University Press, 1994), pp. 24, 34.

56. Ibid., p. 183.

57. *Picayune*, April 7, 1847.

58. James Melvin Lee, *History of American Journalism* (Boston: Houghton Mifflin Company, 1917), pp. 258-62; Robert W. Desmond, *The Information Process* (Iowa City: University of Iowa Press, 1978), pp. 171-76.

59. *Picayune*, November 11, 1846.

60. Livermore, *Review of the Mexican War*, pp. 227-28.

61. Ibid., p. 229.

7.
A View of the Periphery: Regional Factors and Collaboration During the U.S.-Mexico Conflict, 1845-1848

Douglas W. Richmond

Little doubt remains that the regions farthest from Mexico City tended to resist U.S. forces the least during the Mexican War. Collaboration on the Mexican periphery occurred partially because the regional economies of the north and southeast depended greatly upon international trade. When guerrilla activity did take place, the local elite tended to distance themselves from insurrections in order to maintain lucrative trading ties with U.S. customers. Difficult economic conditions motivated those with less means to collaborate with North Americans for financial gain. Collaboration—both "active" and "passive"—occurred throughout Mexico, even in Mexico City.

Historical examples abound. Various alliances during World War IIp   152   152 indicate unusually strong instances of collaboration. The collaboration of Swiss banks with Nazi Germany is now accepted as a conclusive example of a high level of financial exchanges.[1] The participation of diverse Europeans in the German armed forces or with police units represent another form of intense collaboration. For example, the Germans recruited a million and a half Soviet citizens to serve in the Wehrmacht during World War II.[2] Finally, some countries collaborated with Hitler to exterminate Jews, gypsies and other ethnic groups. The most severe Axis regimes, such as those in Croatia and Slovakia, preserved some independence because the policy of extermination dominated Hitler's strategy.[3]

Certainly the collaboration of some Mexicans with the forces of President James K. Polk represent a "passive" alliance compared with certain European nations between 1939 and 1945. Mexican banks were undeveloped and, if only for that reason, there was little financial collaboration. Also, the number of Mexicans recruited to serve in the U.S. armed forces is of comparatively little consequence in spite of various spies and bandits.[4] Concerning a policy of racism with regard to the indigenous population, one can also conclude that many Mexicans feared resident Indians rather than North Americans; consider the caste wars in Yucatán and in the Sierra Gorda.[5]

By 1846, Mexico's sense of national unity had not developed sufficiently for the country's leaders to mobilize the nation against U.S. invasion. The wave of optimism that Mexico enjoyed after gaining its independence from Spain in 1821 was short-lived as bitter political disputes weakened the tenuous fabric of national unity. The resulting political instability meant that seventeen governments—most temporary—ruled Mexico between 1829 and 1837.

Federalism appealed to regions along the southern and northern periphery more than the more conservative central area around Mexico City. Produced by a majority of federalists during the constituent congress that met in November, 1823, the 1824 Constitution enabled the nineteen state governments to enjoy a great deal of autonomy. Each state had sovereign powers within its jurisdiction as a federation of equals. The state governments, in fact, elected formally the president and vice president, even if both candidates represented different political parties. Reflecting Mexico's long colonial experience, the new constitution had no separation of church and state, nor did it mention equality before the law. The legal immunities from civil courts enjoyed by the clergy and military remained. The 1824 Constitution provided a conservative institutional continuity in terms of religion and the armed forces while maximizing regional autonomy.[6]

Three political factions emerged after the 1828 presidential elections: centralists had attempted to revolt against Mexico's first republican president, Guadalupe Victoria, and, in response, the federalists split into moderate and radical factions. Moderates rallied behind

General Manuel Gómez Pedraza, Victoria's minister of war. Radicals supported General Vicente Guerrero, one of the heroes of the independence movement against Spain. Although Gómez Pedraza won the 1828 election, Guerrero revolted and established a populistic regime that attempted to exile all Spaniards. Guerrero's minister of finance, Lorenzo de Zavala, sold church property and decreed a progressive income tax. These events contributed to a deep polemical dispute between the three groups, particularly after conservatives overthrew Guerrero and executed him.[7]

The radical federalist interpretation of the 1824 Constitution limited national defense because it embraced Jeffersonian concepts of a weak confederation whose state governments would preserve funds to defend states rather than national interests against North American threats. Radicals also planned to establish a volunteer civic militia to limit the political influence of the national army.[8] In addition, the radicals wanted to continue mobilizing the urban masses and install a populistic agenda. After the Texas revolt, most federalists pursued a belligerent policy against the United States.

The moderates distrusted the national army but wanted to limit militia forces to property-owning citizens. Most moderates favored a conservative republic that would not cater to the interests of the working masses. They sought restricted free trade and favored a peaceful resolution of differences with the United States, particularly on the Texas issue.

Centralists wanted a strong national government by allying with the church and the regular army. Conservatives restricted social mobility by denying full citizenship to the lower classes. The traditionalists sought to maintain a social system inherited from the colonial period. In general, centralists favored a Hispanic tradition of high tariff protection and distrust of the British as well as the United States. Such sharp differences were intensified by a free press, which all three factions used to subject their enemies to relentless sectarian criticism.[9]

The Yucatán Peninsula and the Southeast

Regional collaboration with U.S. forces weakened Mexican hopes for winning the war. Undoubtedly the most notable example is

Yucatán, which possessed a long history of autonomist sentiments. Yucatán joined the Mexican republic in 1824 only on the basis of unconditional federalism. The federal government's transition to centralism in 1835 and 1836 definitely alienated Yucatán. Forced to pay a sales tax and higher customs tariffs as well as angered by having to send 2500 citizens to fight in the Texas campaign, Yucatán revolted successfully in 1839. Two attempts by the central government to crush Yucatán failed. Texas supported the Yucatecan desire for self-rule. In fact, the Texas Navy departed from Galveston harbor on June 24, 1840, and sailed up the Tabasco River to join a federalist assault on San Juan Bautista, a centralist city. By December, 1841, Texas and Yucatán agreed to an alliance whereby the Texas Navy would prevent a Mexican invasion of Yucatán in return for a rental fee of $8000 a month and an understanding that Yucatán and Texas would divide equally all booty from Mexican ships taken by Yucatecan and Texan vessels.[10] It is not surprising, therefore, that after Yucatán declared its autonomy, John Lloyd Stephens, an explorer whose insights into the Yucatecan past became well known, doubted that the central government could retake Yucatán. "[It] is a limb," he concluded, "forever lopped from that great but feeble and distracted republic."[11]

A complete break from Mexico occurred partially as a result of Mexico City's refusal to honor past agreements. After negotiating a December, 1843, autonomy pact, the Yucatecan elites seemed to have virtual self-rule. But the national governments, whether conservative or moderate, continued to impose trade restrictions upon Yucatán. When the Mexican congress repudiated the 1843 autonomy agreement on December 14, 1845, Yucatán's lawmakers simultaneously decreed their independence and withdrew recognition of the national government two weeks later. After war broke out between the United States and Mexico, the Yucatecan legislature decided that it would arrange internal and international matters as it deemed appropriate. In return for not blockading Yucatecan ports, the U.S. Navy received supplies such as fruit and cattle. But, Yucatán insisted, "as a new testimony to the spirit of nationalism," that it was willing to reunite with Mexico if Mexico would recognize Yucatán's autonomy.[12]

Once again Santa Anna succeeded in promising Yucatán its autonomy in return for its support of his return to power. Santa Anna appealed to Yucatecans because of his decision to restore the 1824 Constitution and his opposition to a monarchical government. Santa Anna left Cuba, where he had been exiled, to meet with Governor Miguel Barbachano in the Yucatecan port of Sisal. After listening to Santa Anna's promises to support autonomy, the legislators declared Yucatán's reincorporation into Mexico on November 7, 1846.[13]

But a month later, the district of Campeche rebelled successfully against the state legislature in Mérida to protect its merchant fleets from U.S. naval forces. Although the elite in Mérida had always insisted that they were staunch federalists, the deputies controlled Yucatán's local affairs with an iron fist. Indigenous communities supported Campeche's demand for tax reductions. More ominously, Campeche insisted that Yucatán remain unconditionally neutral during the war with the United States. In Campeche sentiment persisted that Mexico could not possibly win against the United States and that local exports would be diminished by U.S. blockades of Mexican ports. And Campeche's leadership opposed Yucatán's reincorporation into Mexico.[14] Campeche forces marched victoriously into Mérida in January, 1847.

The United States pressured the new Yucatecan regime to distance itself from the rest of Mexico. After a U.S. warship sailed into Campeche harbor on June 4, 1847, the captain demanded to know Yucatán's intentions during the war. The Mérida government replied that Yucatán had temporarily separated from Mexico.[15] Meanwhile, the U.S. secretary of the navy attempted to win the support of Chiapas and Tabasco. At one point, the state department considered seizing the isthmus of Tehuantepec partially as a means to back any faction in Yucatán that would continue to uphold separation from Mexico.[16] Because former Governor Barbachano had sent supplies to Mexico from Yucatán after his reunification with Mexico, U.S. warships occupied the ports of Carmen and Laguna. Seizing these southeastern ports undoubtedly formed part of the U.S. strategy to attack Veracruz.[17]

The outbreak of a Maya revolt altered Mérida's strategy considerably. As the wholesale slaughter of several hundred thousand inhabitants began, the Maya gained momentum and eventually occupied most of the Yucatecan Peninsula. The new governor's son-in-law, Justo Sierra O'Reilly, pleaded for U.S. assistance to squelch the Maya uprising. Even more desperate, liberal Governor Santiago Méndez offered Yucatecan sovereignty to Spain, Britain and the United States. Local Spaniards raised Spanish flags; later, the Mérida government offered to sell Campeche to Spain. The Europeans declined, but President Polk urged congress to accept Méndez's overture. Polk proposed sending U.S. troops to Yucatán to avoid further bloodshed, restrain European influence, and occupy a region that seemed to be headed by willing collaborators. After it received word that Barbachano had arranged a peace treaty with the Maya, the U.S. congress voted against annexation.[18] Elsewhere in the southeast, the states of Chiapas and Tabasco considered uniting with Guatemala. Tabasco declared a brief separation from Mexico on November 19, 1846.

California and New Mexico

As in the southeast, the centralist state had weak ties with the northern frontier of Mexico. The centralist 1836 Constitution limited the civil autonomy of state governments. Shaky financial conditions and a stream of U.S. immigrants prevented Mexico from maintaining healthy ties to its frontier societies. The upper class in the north profited from U.S. trade while continuing to yearn for federalism. The inability of Mexico to cement relations with states in the far northwest became a critical factor in the war with the United States.

Californians enjoyed a tranquil autonomy while New Mexicans became sullen and divided. In Alta California, one key event was the secularization of the Franciscan missions in 1834. The creation of a large class of rancher/farmers provided economic stability and a less rigid class structure. Local leaders, notably Andrés Pico, perhaps with the aid of his brother Governor Pio Pico, took over missions such as

San Fernando Rey de España in 1834. But it can also be argued, as historian David Weber does, that the collapse of the missions shattered a culturally unifying Hispanic legacy. Moreover, California had never been integrated into the Mexican economy. By the early nineteenth century, California found that it could not depend upon overland trade with New Mexico or through Sonora. Once its destiny appeared to be tied to the sea, ranchers began smuggling cowhides and tallow to foreign traders.[19]

In the 1830s and 1840s, more Anglo-Americans and Europeans settled in California. A small number married into local families and assumed Mexican citizenship. But most of the immigrants were hostile to the Mexican government. In 1846, they declared an independent California republic. Within a month of the so-called Bear Flag Revolt, U.S. forces began to invade California in general. Governor Pio Pico attempted to rally support for his government. Pio Pico requested a key minister, Matias Moreno, to return to his position as Oficial Mayor, or chief of staff, even after Moreno had ignored previous appeals to assume duties "each day more necessary."[20]

Governor Pico also attempted to appeal to fellow *californios* directly. From Santa Barbara, Pio Pico lashed out on June 23 at "North American adventurers" who had invaded Sonoma "with the darkest treason that could be invented." "The North Americans can never be our friends," he intoned, because "they have laws, religion, language, and dress totally the opposite of ours." The embattled governor warned that the "horrible slavery that they permit in their states" as well as the Protestant religion would be the price of defeat.[21] Three days later, Pio Pico's government began to feel "great uncertainness" concerning the June, 1846, events at Sonoma when approximately forty U.S. settlers seized Mexican officials and began the Bear Flag Revolt. Pio Pico ordered subprefects across California to issue proclamations "inviting" male inhabitants to fight "the foreign invasion." But few recruits materialized when Governor Pico ordered the conscription of all males between fifteen and sixty years.[22]

One local official called on the British government for aid against the U.S. rebels. At one o'clock on June 29, 1846, the northern district's prefect reported to the British vice consul that without a declaration of war, U.S. "adventurers" had overpowered Sonoma and raised their flag. The prefect feared that these events "should be considered another robbery like Texas" and predicted correctly that U.S. warships would soon appear. Fearing a U.S. blockade, the official claimed that "The undersigned, satisfied that Great Britain is allied with the Mexican Republic," would no doubt "impart its protection" in the form of sending a British sloop along the California coast. Exhorting the British vice consul not to deny his petition, the prefect concluded that sending a warship "by itself would be enough to impede the progress of the American invasion."[23]

As in other parts of Mexico, guerrillas fought back and even enjoyed temporary success. A U.S. force of less than 100 troops could not control Los Angeles, which was recaptured by José María Flores, a former Mexican officer. Guerrillas also recovered the town of Chino with its U.S. garrison and carried on the fighting to Santa Barbara. In many villages throughout southern California, Mexicans were able to regain control of their communities. Governor Pico fled to Sonora, but his brother Andrés Pico led Mexican forces to their only clear-cut victory during the battle of San Pascual.[24] The San Pascual victory symbolized the tendency of the masses to fight back. But Californians were unique in that they mobilized resistance successfully.

In general, however, the upper class was not interested in confronting the North Americans. Mariano Guadalupe Vallejo provides an example. He was an influential *californio* by the 1840s with landholdings in Sonoma that included large vineyards and productive pastures. In fact, Vallejo's hacienda functioned as the cultural center of the region. By the time the war with the United States became an issue that few could avoid, Vallejo was convinced that only the United States could develop the tremendous potential of California's land and climate. When war broke out, he backed the U.S.[25]

New Mexico also became dissatisfied under Mexican rule. Mexico's ill-fated 1836 attempt to impose a centralized state failed in the north. When Santa Anna appointed an outsider, Albino Pérez, as governor of New Mexico, many citizens refused to cooperate. Most *nuevomexicanos* wanted municipal control of village life in the tradition of the pre-Hispanic indigenous culture. Lack of water and Apache warfare restricted agricultural success throughout the territory. Not until 1843 did the settlement of the fertile Mesilla Valley begin when Pablo Melendes started the Doña Ana Bend Colony. The political turmoil that characterized Mexico after independence from Spain resulted in the abandonment of the missions and presidios while rations to pacify the Apaches dried up. The fierce Athabaskans seemed to be gaining the upper hand by the 1840s in the Tucson area. Not surprisingly, Pérez's moral and financial excesses as well as his imposition of the centralist 1836 Constitution motivated Mexicans and Indians in northern New Mexico to revolt in August, 1837. The rebels killed Pérez and sixteen of his subordinates. After the bloody uprising, Manuel Armijo defeated the rebels by means of inspired generalship and succeeded Pérez as governor.[26]

Given the disillusionment with Mexico City that characterized New Mexico, it is not surprising that the Polk regime needed little effort to recruit collaborators. New Mexico already enjoyed close economic ties to St. Louis and U.S. merchants who resided in Santa Fe as well as other towns throughout the territory. Particularly critical were the roles of George T. Howard and James Wiley Magoffin. Both had become prominent merchants in Santa Fe, partially as a result of their unlimited capacity for alcoholic beverages and for making friends. They each agreed to collect covert intelligence at the request of the U.S. government. Even more crucial was the secretary of the war department's request that Howard and Magoffin persuade Mexican officials and Governor Armijo not to resist U.S. invaders. Proceeding to Santa Fe in an alcoholic stupor, Magoffin led a caravan worth over a million dollars that included thousands of bottles of champagne as well as claret. When Magoffin arrived in Santa Fe under a flag of truce, he persuaded Armijo to withdraw and accept annexation. The Mexican commander at Tucson also withdrew in December, 1846.[27]

Colonel Stephen Kearny enjoyed clear superiority when he received confidential orders to seize New Mexico. His task was so vital that Kearny took Santa Fe on the day that congress declared war against Mexico. Like other U.S. commanders, Kearny added Catholic chaplains to his forces to overcome Mexican fears of uncompromising Protestantism. Kearny also issued a proclamation that U.S. forces would protect civil as well as religious rights. As he moved through New Mexican villages, Kearny swore in officials who would serve him. He also paid for corn stolen by his troops. Kearny even attended a mass and hosted a dance after he entered Santa Fe. In general, the *nuevomexicanos* received U.S. forces warmly. Subsequent guerrilla resistance indicates that the conquest of New Mexico was not blood-less. But many New Mexicans supported U.S. annexation out of their belief that the North American army could control hostile indigenous groups. Kearny substantiated this view by summoning Pueblo leaders to a council at Santa Fe and signing a peace treaty with the Navajos.[28]

Thus Mexico City's inability to maintain relations with the north-ern states farthest from the national capital was a critical factor in its war with the United States.

Events in Baja California

In Baja California outright cooperation between the upper-class Mexicans and U.S. forces provoked a certain amount of lower-class-based guerrilla movements that can almost be characterized as a miniature civil war in the context of a foreign invasion. Baja California reinforces the theme that the Mexican upper class along the periphery profited from U.S. trade while continuing to yearn for federalism.

The U.S. Navy encountered stiff resistance when it invaded Mazatlán, but had little trouble in seizing control of the main ports in Baja California. Under the terms of Baja California's surrender, Governor Francisco Palacios Miranda secured the right to continue having Mexican civil officials serve at their posts. The governor also obtained an agreement whereby the North Americans granted Baja Californians the rights and privileges of U.S. citizens. Had the United States lost interest in annexing Baja California, the collaborators would have offered the peninsula to Great Britain. Even when U.S.

naval authorities announced their intention to maintain possession of
Baja California after the war, several collaborators actively supported
their goal of permanent U.S. occupation.[29]

The issue of the U.S. invasion precipitated sharp class differences
in attitudes about the war. Most of the collaborators in Baja
California were upper class. Troops who served under Palacios
Miranda battled Mexican guerrillas. In ports such as La Paz, nearly all
of the upper class favored U.S. rule. Eventually, about 300 elites had
to leave when Baja California leaders decided to remain with Mexico
after 1848. Extensive guerrilla activity in rural areas or small towns
indicated middle class as well as mass opposition to U.S. hegemony.
On one occasion, pro-Mexican forces entered La Paz and burned the
homes of all those who favored U.S. domination.[30]

Opponents of North American rule faced many obstacles. Almost
from the beginning, they bemoaned the U.S. naval blockade and the
lack of necessary resources. Centralists hoped that Santa Anna, "the
immortal warrior of Tampico and Veracruz" (where he had defeated
Spanish and French attempts to invade Mexico) would restore order.[31]
When guerrilla forces learned that U.S. supplies had fallen into friendly hands, they eagerly appealed for the items.[32] One patriot proudly
sent a barrel of aguardiente "to give the troops a drink at night when
they are tired at the camp after battling the enemy."[33] When guerrillas
overpowered towns such as Todos Santos, they appealed for financial
aid when no funds could be obtained locally.[34] When ordered to attack
nearby U.S. forces, guerrillas sometimes hesitated, requesting information about the numbers of U.S. troops, their arms and their precise
position.[35] Appeals for fresh supplies became critical because many
volunteers were aged patriots. After occupying San Xavier, one guerrilla group asked for aid, perhaps because one soldier was seventy-
three years old.[36] Another guerrilla commander noted that he had
recruited seventy-six fighters but had only twelve rifles; he requested
fifty more.[37]

A wave of democratic nationalism seems to have propelled much
of the opposition to any alliance with U.S. occupation forces. There
is some indication that more than one "popular election" took place

when the rebels swept away constituted authorities.[38] Guerrilla units sometimes based their formation on a national congressional law that called on all able males to take up arms.[39] Irregulars from Camandú announced proudly that they had elected officers in free, spontaneous voting.[40] It is difficult to say if there was any central coordination to the various guerrilla units, but several addressed their communications to territorial juntas, which suggests a very localized movement. Most interpreted the neutrality agreement as a mere façade for U.S. occupation. When *jefes políticos* tried to enforce the neutrality decree, guerrillas opposed them by arguing that such a decision lacked "the knowledge and consent of the people." Rebel leader Manuel Pineda almost captured San José del Cabo early in 1848 until U.S. naval reinforcements arrived. But even partial success encouraged rebel confidence. Pineda noted that U.S. forces "had not stepped one pace from their forts in spite of the inferiority of our weapons and our lack of supplies."[41]

Northern Mexico

Sonora, Chihuahua, Coahuila, Nuevo León, Sinaloa, Durango and Tamaulipas gradually felt estranged from Mexico City. Long a center of federalist sentiment, the northern states had established a lifestyle that left them on the edge of national politics. Merchants in northern and coastal areas profited from free trade rather than protectionism. Smuggling made Monterrey and Pacific coastal regions lucrative commercial areas. Northerners had been accustomed to receiving assistance from the central government to fight Indians but the aid ended after independence. The absence of economic integration and infrastructure, as well as the neglect of colonization projects, led to an eventual decline in allegiance to the national government.[42]

Because many citizens of northern Mexico resented centralism, they often aided U.S. military operations. Particularly notable is Chapita Sandoval, who reported the correct strength of General Mariano Arista's forces at Matamoros to General Zachary Taylor in August, 1845. Also, General William J. Worth received valuable information on the defense of Monterrey from Mexican spies.[43] In addition to treating the U.S. forces with "great hospitality," as correspondent George Kendall reported from Parras, some upper-class Mexicans were not reluctant to sell supplies to U.S. commanders.[44] Peons became friendly with North Americans because they could work for U.S. soldiers and be paid enough to cast off debt obligations to masters, as occurred in Camargo where there was a demand for labor.[45] One startled U.S. soldier learned that many Mexicans were reluctant to make peace because they prospered from sales of goods as well as employment.[46] U.S. forces throughout northeastern Mexico acted as a magnet, attracting thousands of unemployed laborers.[47]

Women also collaborated with U.S. forces actively. U.S. soldiers easily found Mexican females to wash laundry and cook. Sexual liasons became fairly common. Other women nursed sick, wounded, and dying U.S. soldiers. Recognizing the potential economic rewards of doing business with U.S. forces, many wealthy Mexican females provided hospitality and goods to the invaders.[48]

Local governments in northern Mexico shunned association with Mexico City. The independent Yucatecan legislature corresponded cordially with the governments of Chihuahua, Tamaulipas, Sonora, Michoacán, Sinaloa, and Zacatecas. Yucatán's proud assertions of autonomy and suggestions that the north follow suit did not fall on deaf ears.[49] After the federal government proclaimed a national draft of 30,000 males in September, 1846, each state received a quota of men who had to serve. None of the northern states furnished the number assigned them. Only five states in all of Mexico provided the soldiers requested and all of them were in central Mexico.[50]

Several occupied cities in the north established a sullen but pragmatic relationship with U.S. authorities. In Saltillo, Mexican officials preferred negotiation over issues such as the sale of food and alcohol, the nature of martial law, and undisciplined volunteer forces. Resolutions satisfied both sides. Within a few weeks, for instance, Saltillo held municipal elections, enjoyed religious festivals as well as bullfights and considered a general amnesty for those who had resisted U.S. forces. Matamoros, like several other cities, enjoyed greater prosperity once it came into contact with U.S. markets. Expanded trade, discouraged by centralists, served U.S. needs because increased municipal revenues benefited the financial needs of the U.S. military.[51]

Guerrilla activity in the north certainly did not exceed local resistance in California or New Mexico. Very few citizens ever joined officially sanctioned guerrilla units, particularly in Tamaulipas where none answered the call to assemble in Ciudad Victoria or San Luis Potosí. Guerrillas in the north preferred local leaders rather than governors in state capitals. Another factor that weakened overall resistance in the north was antipathy toward federal military commanders appointed in Mexico City. In Monterrey news that national leaders had sent an unpopular Sonoran general to command local forces reduced morale considerably. In Sinaloa, the national government sent Rafael Tellez to lead the fight against the United States. Instead, Tellez simply took over the state and established his own personal *cacicazgo*, or fiefdom, with the aid of foreign merchants.[52]

One item that particularly motivated collaboration was Taylor's March 31, 1847, proclamation that Mexican governments in the occupied zones would have to pay indemnities for the value of goods lost in attacks on wagon trains. Local authorities, therefore, sometimes apprehended suspected guerrillas, particularly when U.S. soldiers came under attack. As part of an ultimately successful anti-guerrilla operation during the fall of 1847, General Wool required local Mexican authorities to ferret out combatants and turn them over to U.S forces. If they did not comply, an entire village would be held responsible. Moreover, those paying taxes to guerrillas would have their goods confiscated. Eventually Wool concluded that if U.S. authorities provided sufficient guarantees of support, several northern states might be persuaded into declaring their independence and perhaps forming an independent nation.[53]

Northerners particularly appreciated the ability of U.S. troops to subdue hostile indigenous groups. As Alexander Doniphan's troops marched into Coahuila, a prominent landowner near Parras asked them to retaliate against Lipan Apaches who had killed several Mexicans and had stolen mules and horses. About thirty of

Doniphan's men ambushed forty or fifty Indians, killing at least half.[54] Such actions undoubtedly encouraged collaboration on every level of society. U.S. troops in Zacatecas also protected local inhabitants from Comanches.[55] By the early 1840s, the Mexican will to resist hostile Indians appears to have diminished seriously. As one U.S. observer noted in Chihuahua, when faced with attacks, the Mexicans "fall on their knees and call on Jesus and Mary and just let them [the Indians] butcher them."[56] A Texas Ranger claimed that Mexican males ran away when Comanches approached, leaving women and children unprotected. When the danger passed, they returned, "braggadocio-like, swear vengeance, threatening to exterminate the tribe...and... pretend to give chase."[57] The presence of U.S. troops, however, promoted joint operations against hostile tribes.[58]

Sentiment for annexing northern Mexico existed in several areas within the United States. In July, 1846, the Cincinnati *Daily Enquirer* clamored for the conquest of northern Mexico in order to give *norteños* "the blessings of political emancipation." The *Daily Enquirer* further proposed ousting the "military despotism under which the provinces groan, and leave the people, so long oppressed by the creatures of the central government, the free choices of their institutions and rulers." Such fanciful generalizations led to a robust but aggressive conclusion: Should these people choose "the Stars and Stripes— so be it!" The paper advocated giving the northern states autonomy if annexation was not possible. In announcing its support of Polk, the *Daily Enquirer* roared, "If this is conquest, then so be it." A year later, the *Daily Enquirer* concluded that the Mexican mind "has become so subdued that it is willing at last to reason calmly and with dignity about the war and its termination."[59]

Various southern leaders echoed a desire to acquire northern Mexico. Representative Jefferson Davis proposed the acquisition of Tamaulipas, Nuevo León, Coahuila and parts of Chihuahua. "Extremist Democrats" proposed annexing all of northern Mexico. Polk and Secretary of State James Buchanan envisioned a Sierra Madre partition, although Polk feared such expansion would require continued war.[60]

United States Forces in Central Mexico

As U.S. soldiers advanced from the frontier into central Mexico, the factors that led to collaboration changed. Local officials who came under occupation continued to work out agreeable arrangements with U.S. officers. Although reduced to a municipal council, Veracruz administrators appointed by U.S. occupation authorities quickly legislated reduced export taxes on goods destined for overseas markets. They also cut import taxes and abolished the tobacco monopoly.[61] Unlike Baja California and Yucatán, collaboration tended to be local and personalized rather than governmental. Moreover, guerrilla resistance weakened in states like Veracruz, Puebla, and Tlaxcala. Several states, notably Guanajuato, refused to send national-guard units outside their local boundaries. As in much of Mexico, Guanajuato authorities placed more attention on maintaining internal order than fighting the invasion.[62]

After arriving in Puebla from Veracruz, General Winfield Scott made good use of bandits and other collaborators. Scott hired bandits to spy for him and paid other highwaymen to protect U.S. forces moving into Puebla. Eventually Scott's intelligence officer formed about 200 criminals, merchants and other collaborators into companies of spies for $20 per man each month. From them, Scott received accurate information about Mexico City's defenses. The spies also fought Mexican guerrillas and skirmished with Santa Anna's forces near Mexico City.[63]

Central Mexico was unique because of the various attempts to form vague confederations in order to reduce, if not eliminate, ties with Mexico City. When Jalisco's leaders proposed a coalition of states to preserve the federalist ideal towards the end of 1846, Querétaro, Aguascalientes and Zacatecas approved while San Luis Potosí, whose civilian leaders suffered from acrimonious relations with federal army commanders, questioned the decision.[64] Other states— Puebla, Veracruz, Querétaro, Michoacán, Guanajuato and Durango—joined Zacatecas in opposing a January 11, 1847, decree that was a forced loan on the church properties and assets. The decree closely resembled a similar action taken by Spain in 1804. It

Engraving of *Winfield Scott, General-in-Chief of the Armies of the United States*. New York: Johnson, Fry, & Co., 1858. (Mexican War Graphics Collection, Special Collections Division, The University of Texas at Arlington Libraries, Arlington, Texas.)

hurt property owners and others who had borrowed from the church to establish businesses, ranches and farms. Had the decree been implemented, thousands would have been bankrupted.[65] Finally, Zacatecas proposed that the coalition replace the federal government and negotiate a quick end to the war because local leaders in small towns and deep within the mountains now defied many state governments and opposed conscription. By January, 1848, the new San Luis Potosí governor asked his legislature to "reassume its sovereignty" apart from the national government.[66]

The fading loyalty of those states between Mexico City and the north played into the hands of U.S. policy makers. Was there any collaboration involved between the north-central coalition-minded states? No evidence has come to light, but the Spanish minister to Mexico did report that Zacatecas, Durango, Sinaloa, and Tabasco wanted to form separate republics under the protection and support of the United States.[67] Individual U.S. soldiers reported that sentiment existed among powerful leaders to have Coahuila annexed to the United States.[68]

The arrival of U.S. forces into the nation's capital came at a time when influential Mexicans were very apprehensive. Once again, Mexican officials decided to cooperate with the North Americans. During his occupation of Mexico City, Winfield Scott purchased the services of a member of the Mexico City municipal government for thirteen weeks. Scott relied on local officials to deal with Mexican matters while U.S. military commissioners handled items involving U.S. interests. The policy worked and provided a certain amount of stability as well as flexibility. Feeding and entertaining the U.S. garrison provided employment for many during a time of desperation. Gradually upper-class Mexicans invited U.S. officers to their homes as well as to substantial social functions. Despite the opposition of the Mexican federal government to elections held in U.S.-occupied areas, residents of the capital appreciated the decision by ocupation forces to permit municipal elections at the end of 1847. To show their gratitude, the newly elected *asamblea municipal* invited U.S. military leaders to a lavish dinner at the nearby Desierto de los Leones in January,

1848. The outing included the finest wines and musical entertainment but provoked criticism from the masses.[69]

As the war came to an end, many disturbing events outside Mexico City encouraged collaborationist sentiments. The caste war in the Sierra Gorda intensified when Mexican army deserters joined angry Indians and local dissidents. At one point, mine workers appealed for direct U.S. annexation. Add these factors to the upper-class fear of continual guerrilla activity or even civil war, and it is not surprising that collaborators in the capital appealed for the incorporation of Mexico into the United States. Some went so far as to offer leadership of the nation to General Scott.[70] As if to justify these fears, disorder plagued the countryside for several years after the war. In Baja California, mass-based militias seized control of several villages in 1849, motivating many to flee because of the allegedly arbitrary manner in which many of the militia units conducted themselves.[71]

The withdrawal of U.S. forces particularly concerned Mariano Otero, minister of external and internal relations in the regime that succeeded Santa Anna and ratified the Treaty of Guadalupe Hidalgo. Otero supported the announcement by several U.S. soldiers to remain in Mexico after the end of the war. Otero thought that U.S. veterans could be useful in case of "whatever disorder." The Mexican president had expressed his hopes to Otero that he expected U.S. forces to provide additional security to populated areas as they left. The federal government, like many of the regional regimes, had a distinct distrust of its own soldiers and citizens.[72] On the other hand, U.S. forces began to sell their weapons as they departed, which provoked fear among the moderates that political rivals could obtain the equipment.[73] As U.S. forces left, Otero tried to stop all public gatherings, "that could produce whatever unrest."[74] Expressing the need for a strong national guard to preserve order, Otero was apprehensive about the rise of theft and overall crime that had occurred in the early summer of 1848.[75] In addition, the moderate government was anxious to receive three million pesos as agreed to by the Treaty of Guadalupe. Otero needed U.S. troops to safeguard the transfer of funds.[76] Mexico's future was indeed uncertain after the devastating conflict, and it is ironic that the national government depended on departing U.S. forces to maintain order. A bitterly divided Mexico continued to teeter on the brink of civil war.

Yet the issues that had weakened the nation during the war revealed themselves as the North Americans packed their bags. As can be seen, the masses were eager for steady work and burdened by the high cost of social services. The indigenous peoples of Mexico revolted openly in the south and central regions of the country. It would be decades before the country would unite politically; not until the twentieth century would egalitarianism become official rhetoric.

NOTES

1. Arthur L. Smith, Jr., *Hitler's Gold: The Story of the Nazi War Loot* (Oxford: St. Marin's Press, 1996); Tom Bower, *Nazi Gold*, rev. ed. (New York: HarperPerennial, 1998).

2. Carlos Caballero Jurado and Kevin Lyles, *Foreign Volunteers of the Wehrmacht, 1941-1945* (London: Osprey, 1983); Nina Tumarkin, *The Living and the Dead: The Rise and Fall of the Cult of World War II in Russia* (New York: Basic Books, 1994), pp. 86-88, 97, 116, 123; Earl F. Ziemke, *Stalingrad to Berlin: The German Defeat in the East* (Washington, D.C.: U.S. Army Center of Military History, 1968).

3. Donald D. Wall, *Nazi Germany and World War II* (St. Paul: West Pulishing Company, 1997), pp. 198-220; Michael J. Lyons, *World War II: A Short History*, 2nd ed. (Englewood Cliffs, New Jersey: Prentice Hall, 1994), pp. 125-37; Michael R. Marrus, *The Holocaust in History* (New York: New American Library, 1989), pp. 75-83.

4. A. Brooke Caruso, *The Mexican Spy Company: United States Covert Operations in Mexico, 1845-1848* (Jefferson, North Carolina: McFarland, 1991).

5. Nelson Reed, *The Caste War of Yucatan* (Stanford: Stanford University Press, 1964); William B. Taylor, *Drinking, Homicide and Rebellion in Colonial Mexican Villages* (Stanford: Stanford University Press, 1979), pp. 113-51. Jean Meyer, *Problemas campesinas y revueltas agrarias, 1821-1910* (Mexico City: Sepseteatas, 1973), pp. 1-67; Leticia Reina, "The Sierra Gorda Peasant Rebellion, 1847-50," in Friedrich Katz, ed., *Riot, Rebellion, and Revolution* (Princeton: Princeton University Press, 1988), pp. 269-94; Terry L. Rugeley, *Yucatan's Maya Peasantry and the Origins of the Caste War* (Austin: University of Texas Press, 1996);

Douglas W. Richmond, "Colaboración entre mexicanos y norteamericanos durante la guerra del 47," paper presented at the Biblioteca Nacional in Mexico City on September 24, 1996. For a broad application of guerrilla warfare, see Gilberto López y Rivas, *La guerra del 47 y la resistencia popular a la ocupación* (Mexico City: Editorial Nuestro Tiempo, 1976).

6. An excellent statistical revision of early political chaos is Donald Fithian Stevens, *Origins of Instability in Early Republican Mexico* (Durham: Duke University Press, 1991), which argues that Mexico became unstable because of the contradictions between liberalism and Mexico's traditional class structure as well as the authoritarian colonial heritage. Although Stanley G. Green's *The Mexican Republic: The First Decade, 1823-1832* (Pittsburgh: University of Pittsurgh Press, 1986) is somewhat lacking in terms of identifying the actual political movements, it provides a wealth of information on various topics. Jan Bazant discusses the 1824 Constitution in his "From Independence to the Liberal Republic, 1821-1867," in Leslie Bethell, ed., *Mexico Since Independence* (New York: Cambridge University Press, 1991), pp. 9-10. For the formulation of the 1824 Constitution, see Timothy E. Anna, "Inventing Mexico: Provincehood and Nationhood after Independence," *Bulletin of Latin American Research*, vol. 15 (Jan. 1996), pp. 8-17.

7. For the attempted expulsion of the Spaniards, see Romeo Flores Caballero, *Counterrevolution: The Role of the Spaniards in the Independence of Mexico, 1804-1838* (Lincoln: University of Nebraska Press, 1974). Also helpful are Jaime Rodríguez O., "The Conflict Between Church and State in Early Republican Mexico," *New World*, vol. 2 (1987), pp. 93-112 and Michael Costeloe, *Church Wealth in Mexico* (Cambridge: Cambridge University Press, 1967), as well as C. Harvey Gardiner, *Mexico, 1825-1828* (Chapel Hill: University of North Carolina Press, 1959). Josefina Zoraida Vázquez, "Political Plans and Collaboration Between Civilians and the Military," *Bulletin of Latin American Research*, vol. 15 (Jan. 1996), pp. 19-38, is also revealing.

8. Pedro Santoni, "The Failure of Mobilization: The Civic Militia of Mexico in 1846," *Mexican Studies/Estudios Mexicanos*, vol. 12 (Summer, 1996), pp. 169-94.

9. The newest and clearest interpretation of the domestic political standoff between the three factions is Pedro Santoni, *Mexicans at Arms: Puro Federalists and the Politics of War, 1845-1848* (Fort Worth: Texas Christian University Press, 1996). Also see Jesús Velasco Marquez's superb "La separacion y anexión de Texas en la historia de Mexico," in Josefina Zoraida Vázquez, ed., *De la rebelión de Texas a la guerra del 47* (Mexico City: Nueva Imagen, 1995), pp. 125-66. Another interpretation is Josefina Zoraida Vázquez, ed., *La fundación del Estado Mexicano* (Mexico City: Nueva Imagen, 1995).

10. Howard F. Cline, "Regionalism and Society in Yucatan, 1825-1847," in *Related Studies in Early Nineteenth Century Yucatecan Social History* (Chicago: University of Chicago Library, 1955), p. 67; Albino Acereto, *Evolución Histórica de las relaciones políticas entre Mexico y Yucatán* (Mexico City: Imprenta Muller hnos., 1907), p. 69; Reed, *The Caste War of Yucatan*, pp. 27-32. For the role of the Texas Navy see Alexander Dienst, "The Navy of the Republic of Texas, III" *The Quarterly of the Texas State Historical Association*, vol. 13 (1909-1910), pp. 18-28; Tom Henderson Wells, *Commodore Moore and the Texas Navy* (Austin: University of Texas Press, 1960), pp. 30-58; Jim Don Hill, *The Texas Navy* (New York: A.S. Barnes, 1937), pp. 130-45.

11. John Lloyd Stephens, *Incidents of Travel in Central America, Chiapas, and Yucatan* (Washington, D.C.: Smithsonian Institution Press, 1993), p. 236.

12. For a summary of these events, see Douglas W. Richmond, "Yucatán's Struggle for Sovereignty during the Mexican-U.S. Conflict, 1836-1848," in Richard Sanchez, Eric Van Young and Gisela Von Wobesser, eds., *La ciudad y el campo en la historia de México* (Mexico City: Universidad Nacional Autónoma de México, Instituto de Investigaciones Históricas, 1992), pp. 173-83. For Yucatecan supplies, see Stanley J. Adamiak, "American Naval Logistics during the Mexican War, 1846-1848," *Military History of the West*, vol. 28 (Spring, 1998), pp. 8-9.

13. Quoted in Yucatecan Documents (hereafter cited as YD), Sesiones del Congreso (hereafter cited as SC), Special Collections, Library of the University of Texas at Arlington, Roll 29, vol. 16, frames 13-14. Ramón Osorio y Carvajal, *Yucatán en las luchas libertarias de México* (Puebla: Editorial J.M. Cajica, Jr., 1972), p. 164, confirms the meeting in Sisal between Santa Anna and Barbachano.

14. YD/SC, Roll 38, vol. 14, frames 26-27; Juan Suárez y Navarro, *Informe sobre las causas y carácter de las frecuentes cámbios políticos occuridos en el estado de Yucatán* (Mexico City: Impr. de I. Cumplido, 1861), pp. 10, 18; Acereto, *Evolución histórica de las relaciones*, pp. 85-88. For an excellent discussion of the differences between Campeche and Mérida, see Lorena Careaga Viliesid, "Neutralidad y rebellión: Yucatán entre dos guerras, 1846-1849," in Laura Herrera Serna, *México en guerra (1846-1848) Perspectivas regionales* (Mexico City: Consejo Nacional para la Cultura y los Artes, Museo Nacional de las Intervenciones, 1997), pp. 673-98.

15. Francis Joseph Manno, "Yucatán en la guerra entre México y Estados Unidos," *Revista de la Universidad de Yucatán*, vol. 5 (julio-agosto, 1963), pp. 51-72.

16. C.H. Gibbon to James Buchanan, Secretary of State, July 22, 1846, *Correspondence of the United States Department of State Miscellaneous Letters, July 1 to Dec. 30, 1846* (Washington D.C.: Government Printing Office, 1946), Microcopy 179, Roll 111, Frames 89-90.

17. *La Patria*, July 30, 1846; Mary W. Williams, "Secessionist Diplomacy of Yucatán," *Hispanic American Historical Review*, vol. 9 (1929), p. 135.

18. Justo Sierra O'Reilly, *Diario de nuestro viaje a los Estados Unidos* (Mexico City: Antigua Libreria Robredo, 1938), pp. 33-50; Williams, "Secessionist Diplomacy of Yucatán," pp. 137-141; María Cecilia Zulueta, "Yucatán y la guerra con Estados Unidos: ¿Una neutalidad anunciada?" in Josefina Zoraida Vázquez, *México al tiempo de su guerra con Estados Unidos, 1846-1848* (Mexico City: Fondo de Cultura Economica, 1997), pp. 609-10.

19. David J. Weber, *The Mexican Frontier, 1821-1846: The American Southwest Under Mexico*. (Albuquerque: University of New Mexico Press, 1982) and Leonard Pitt, *The Decline of the Californios* (Berkeley: University of California Press, 1966) are key sources.

20. Governor Pio Pico to Matias Moreno, April 22, 1846, Centro de Estudios de Historia de México, Mexico City (hereinafter cited as CEHM), Fondo DCC-CLVIII-1-56, no. 32.

21. Proclamation of Governor Pio Pico from Santa Barbara, June 23, 1846, CEHM, Fondo DCCCLVIII-1-59, no. 34.

22. Quoted in A.T. Coronel to Matias Moreno, June 26, 1846, CEHM, Fondo DCCCLVIII-1-58, no. 33; the Bear Flag revolt is noted in John Charles Fremont, *Memoirs of My Life* (Chicago: Clarke and company, 1887), p. 520. Conscription is noted in Jack Bauer, *The Mexican War* (Lincoln: University of Nebrasaka Press, 1992), p. 172.

23. Comandancia General, Prefectura del Segundo Distrito to Diego Forbes, British vice consul, June 29, 1846, CEHM, Fondo DCCCLVIII-1-61, no. 35.

24. Pitt, *Decline of the Californios*, pp. 33-35; Bauer, *The Mexican War*, p. 183; Albert Camarillo, *Chicanos in a Changing Society: From Mexican Pueblos to American Barrios in Santa Barbara and Southern California, 1848-1930* (Cambridge: Harvard University Press, 1979), p. 13. A fine overview is Antonio Rios Bustamante, "La resistancía popular en Alta California durante la guerra entre Mexico y Estados Unidos, 1846-1848," in Herrera Serna, *México en guerra*, pp. 117-29.

25. Alan Rosenus, *General M.G. Vallejo and the Advent of the Americans* (Albuquerque: University of New Mexico Press, 1995) is a compelling biography of a collaborator who eventually lost much of his estate to greedy Anglo-Americans.

26. Janet Lecompte, *Rebellion in Rio Arriba, 1837* (Albuquerque: University of New Mexico Press, 1985); Thomas E. Sheridan, *Los Tucsonenses: The Mexican*

Community in Tucson, 1854-1941 (Tucson: Universiy of Arizona Press, 1986), pp. 13-26; Paxton P. Price, *Pioneers of the Mesilla Valley* (Las Cruces: Yucca Tree Press, 1995).

27. Caruso, *The Mexican Spy Company*; pp. 94-103; Thomas E. Chávez, *Manuel Alvarez, 1794-1856: A Southwestern Biography* (Niwot, Colorado: University Press of Colorado, 1990); Sheridan, *Los Tucsonenses*, pp. 23-25; Martín González de la Vara, "Los nuevomexicanos ante la invasión norteamericano, 1846-1848," in Herrera Serna, *México en guerra*, pp. 473-94.

28. Bauer, *The Mexican War*, pp. 128-37; Robert M. Utley, *The Indian Frontier of the American West, 1846-1848* (Albuquerque: University of New Mexico Press, 1984), pp. 39-46; Governor Charles Bent to Secretary of State James Buchanan, Oct. 15, 1846, in "Navajos in New Mexico," Box GA159, Special Collections Division, University of Texas at Arlington; John T. Hughes, *Doniphan's Expedition: An Account of the U.S. Army Operations in the Great American Southwest* (Cincinnati: J.A. And U.P. James, 1848), pp. 185-206; Douglas W. Richmond, "Climax of Spanish, Mexican, and U.S. Conflicts with Native Americans in New Mexico: Treaty Making and the U. S.-Mexican War, 1846-1848," manuscript under review by the *New Mexico Historical Review*.

29. Bauer, *The Mexican War*, pp. 345-50; T. J. Farnham, *Life, Adventures, and Travel in California* (New York: Nafis S. Cornish, 1849), p. 429. Also helpful is F. Javier Gaxiola, *La invasion Norte Americano en Sinaloa: Revista Historica del Estado, de 1845 a 1849*, 2 vols. (Mexico City: Antonio Rosas, 1891). Angela Moyano Pahissa, "La invasión norteamericana de Baja California, durante la guerra de 1846-1848" in Herrera Serna, *Mexico en guerra*, p. 140.

30. Bauer, *The Mexican War*, pp. 343-50; Doyce B. Nunis, Jr., ed. *The Mexican War in Baja California: The Memorandum of Captain Henry W. Halleck Concerning His Expedition in Lower California, 1846-1848* (Los Angeles: Dawson's Book Shop, 1977); Moyano Patissa, "La Invasión norteamericana de Baja California," p. 138.

31. Vicente Sotomayor to national government by means of governor of Alta California, Sept. 29, 1846, CEHM, Fondo DCCCLVIII-1-65, no. 36.

32. Guerrilla commander to Nepomencio Castillo, Nov. 11, 1847, CEHM, Fondo DCCCLVIII-1-73, no. 41.

33. José Matías Moreno to Mauricio Castro, Nov. 29, 1847, CEHM, Fondo DCC-CLVIII-1-80, no. 44.

34. Mauricio Castro to Victoriano Legaspi, Dec. 20, 1847, CEHM, Fondo DCC-CLVIII-1-84, no. 46. Rebels in Muleje and Comandú met in Santa Anita where

they declared Mauricio Castro to be Baja California's new political ruler and that Manuel Pineda would lead rebel military forces.

35. Guerrilla commander to Juez Constitucional del Pueblo de Todos Santos, Nov. 8, 1847, CEHM, Fondo DCCCLVIII-1-75, no. 42.

36. Juan Gomez to Matias Moreno, Oct. 8 and 12, 1847, CEHM, Fondo DCC-CLVIII-1-69, 1-72, no. 39, 40.

37. Guerrilla commander to territorial military command, Oct. 7, 1847, CEHM, Fondo DCCCLVIII-1-68, no. 38.

38. Village of Santa Anita to Comandancia Política de la Baja California, Jan. 23, 1848, CEHM, Fondo DCCCLVIII-1-88, no. 48.

39. Guerrilla leader to Comandante General de este territorio, Oct. 7, 1847, CEHM, DCCCLVIII-1-68, no. 38.

40. Guerrilla manifesto from village of Comandú, Oct. 5, 1847, CEHM, Fondo DCCCLVIII-1-66, no. 37.

41. Manuel Pineda, commander of guerrilla forces in San Antonio, to Charles Heywood, commander of U.S. forces in San José, Jan. 28, 1848, CEHM, DCC-CLVIII-1-89, no. 49. Pineda was eventually wounded and captured while Mauricio Castro surrendered, weakening the rebel movement considerably.

42. Stuart Voss, On the Periphery of Nineteenth Century Mexico: Sonora and Sinaloa, 1810-1847 (Tucson: University of Arizona Press, 1982). Lack of national unity is emphasized in Gene Brack, Mexico Views Manifest Destiny, 1846-1848: An Essay on the Origins of the Mexican War (Albuquerque: University of New Mexico Press, 1975), p. 171.

43. Caruso, The Mexican Spy Company, pp. 80-92.

44. The New Orleans Picayune, April 11, 1848; Bauer, The Mexican War, pp. 149-51, 222; Charles H. Harris, III, A Mexican Family Empire: The Latifundia of the Sanchez Navarros, 1765-1867 (Austin: University of Texas Press, 1975), pp. 285-89, notes the activities of this family, the largest employer in the region as does Cecilia Sheridan Prieto in "Coahuila y la invasión norteamericana" in Zoraida Vázquez, México al tiempo de su guerra," pp. 175-78. Joseph Chance, Mexico Under Fire (Fort Worth: Texas Christian University Press, 1994), notes that even Spanish merchants profited from their eagerness to do business with U.S. units.

45. Chance, Mexico Under Fire, p. 127.

46. Douglas W. Richmond, "Andrew Trussell in Mexico: A Soldier's Wartime Impressions, 1847-1848," in Douglas W. Richmond, ed., *Essays on the Mexican War* (College Station: Texas A&M University Press, 1986), pp. 97-99.

47. Migual Angel Gonzáles Quiroga, "Nuevo León ante la invasión norteamericana, 1846-1848," in Herrera Serna, *México en guerra*, pp. 468-69.

48. Ibid., pp. 95-96; Peggy Jeanne Cashion, "Women and the Mexican War," M.A. thesis, University of Texas at Arlington, 1990.

49. YD/SC, Roll 37, Vol. 13, frames 8, 13, 46, 73-74; Manno, "Yucatán en la guerra entre México y Estados Unidos," p. 62.

50. William A. DePalo, Jr., *The Mexican National Army, 1822-1852* (College Station: Texas A&M University Press, 1997), pp. 108-09.

51. Sheridan Prieto, "Coahuila y la invasión norteamericana," pp. 184-86; Juan Fidel Zorrilla, Octavio Herrera Pérez and Maibel Miró Flaquear, "Presencia del ayuntamiento de Matamoros durante la intervención norteamerica de 1847," in Herrera Serna, *México en guerra*, p. 621.

52. Octavio Herrera Pérez, "Tamaulipas ante la guerra de invasión norteamericana," in Zoraida Vazquez, *México al tiempo de su guerra*, pp. 538, 553; Miguel A. González Quiroga, "Nuevo León ocupado: El gobierno de Nuevo León durante la guerra entre México y los Estados Unidos," in Zoraida Vázquez, *Mexico al tiempo de su guerra* p. 344; Carlos Maciel Sánchez, "Pugnas y acomodos políticos en Sinaloa durante la invervención norteamericana," in Herrera Serna, *México en guerra*, pp. 565-579.

53. Bauer, *The Mexican War*, pp. 201-25. *Boletin Republicano de Jalisco*, num. 10, Guadalajara, June 23, 1846, contains editorials expressing the Mexican army's point of view, which were often critical of civilian authorities. Chance, *Mexico Under Fire*, contains other good examples of northern collaboration on pp. 114-25.

54. A Wislizenus, *Memoir: Or a Tour to Northern Mexico Connected with Col. Doniphan's Expedition in 1846-1847* (Washington: Tippin and Streeper, printers, 1848), p. 71.

55. Richmond, "Andrew Trussell in Mexico," p. 97.

56. A. Russell Buchanan, "George Washington Trahern: Texas Cowboy Soldier from Mier to Buena Vista," *Southwestern Historical Quarterly*, vol. 64 (July 1954), p. 89.

57. Samuel C. Reid, *The Scouting Expeditions of McCulloch's Texas Rangers; or, the Summer and Fall Campaign of the Army of the United States in Mexico—1846* (Freeport: Books for Libraries Press, 1970), p. 72.

58. Wislizenus, *Memoir*, p. 53.

59. *Daily Enquirer* (Cincinnati, Ohio), July 28, 30, 1846, July 2, 1847.

60. Paul Horgan, *Great River: The Rio Grande in North American History* (New York: Holt, Rinehart and Winston, 1954), p. 780.

61. Carmen Bláquez Domínguez, "Veracruz: Restablecimiento del federalismo e intervención norteamericana," in Zoraida Vázquez, *México al tiempo de su guerra*, pp. 576-77.

62. José Antonio Serrano Ortega, "Hacienda y Guerra, elites políticas y gobierno nacional: Guanajuato, 1835-1847," in Zoraida Vázquez, *México al tiempo de su guerra*, pp. 244-58. National guard units generally fell under the control of state governments.

63. Caruso, *The Mexican Spy Company*, pp. 147-56.

64. Tomás Calvillo Unna and María Isabel Monroy Castillo, "Entre regionalismo y federalismo: San Luis Potosí, 1846-1848," in Zoraida Vázquez, "*México al tiempo de su guerra*, pp. 431-47, is valuable for regional discontent.

65. Mercedes de Vega, "Puros y moderados: Un obastáculo para la defensa nacional, Zacatecas: 1846-1848," in Zoraida Vázquez, *México al tiempo de su guerra*, pp. 631-32.

66. Cavillo Unna and Monroy Castillo, "Entre regionalismo y federalismo," pp. 450-52.

67. de Vega, "Puros y moderados," pp. 634-35.

68. Richmond, "Andrew Trussel in Mexico," p. 98.

69. María Gayón Córdova, "Los invasores yanquis en la ciudad de México," in Herrera Serna, *Mexico en guerra*, pp. 195-230. See also Bauer, *The Mexican War*, pp. 321-27; Caruso, *The Mexican Spy Company*, pp. 157-58.

70. Bauer, *The Mexican War*, pp. 383-84. The fullest discussion of the Sierra Gorda insurrection is Reina, "The Sierra Gorda Peasant Rebellion," pp. 269-94. It is also mentioned in Paul Vanderwood, *Disorder and Progress: Bandits, Police and Mexican Development* (Lincoln: University of Nebraska Press, 1981), pp. 28-30, and Meyer, *Problemas campesinos y revueltras agrarias*, pp. 13-14.

71. Gabriel González to Agustin Mansillas, CEHM, Fondo DCCCLVIII-1-91, no. 51.

72. Mariano Otero to Luis Cuevas, June 9, 1848, CEHM, Manuscritos de Luis Cuevas, Fondo XVII-3, carpeta 6; Gayón Córdova, "Los invasores yanquis," p. 231; Luis Jáuregui, "Chihuahua en la tormenta, su situación política durante la guerra con los Estados Unidos, septiembre de 1846-julío de 1848," in Zoraida Vázquez, *México al tiempo de su guerra*, p. 154.

73. Otero to Cuevas, June 8, 1848, CEHM, Fondo XVII-3, carpeta 6.

74. Otero to Cuevas, June 7, 1848, CEHM, Fondo XVII-3, carpeta 6.

75. Ibid.

76. Otero to Cuevas, June 9, 1848, CEHM, Fondo XVII-3, carpeta 6.

8.

Young America and the War with Mexico

by Robert W. Johannsen

On March 4, 1845, a cold rainy day in Washington, D.C., James Knox Polk stood on the east portico of the capitol, sheltered by an umbrella, and read his inaugural address. At age forty-nine, he was still not used to the unexpected turn of fortune that had brought him his party's nomination and his defeat of Henry Clay, one of the country's most respected and experienced leaders, in the 1844 election. In his remarks, he moved beyond the usual recital of the principles that would guide his administration to address the meaning America had for him. "This heaven-favored land," he declared, enjoyed the "most admirable and wisest system of well-regulated self-government...ever devised by human minds" wherein...the fire of liberty, warmed "the hearts of happy millions" and invited "all the nations of the earth to imitate our example." Under the benign influence of their republican government, the American people were "free to improve their own condition by the legitimate exercise of all their mental and physical powers," and were "permitted collectively and individually to seek their own happiness in their own way." "Who shall assign limits," Polk asked, "to the achievements of free minds and free hands under the protection of this glorious Union?"[1]

It was a ringing statement of faith by the youngest president of a youthful nation. Many of the elements of what America's romantics called the spirit of the age were echoed in Polk's remarks: the providential dispensation, the appeal to the hearts of the people, the freedom of the individual within a system of popular self-government, the absence of limits to the capacity of individuals to improve themselves. The sentiments were not new, but it was only as the country approached the mid-point of the nineteenth century that they became an article of national faith.

Ralph Waldo Emerson, one of the spokesmen of romantic America, preached a gospel of hope and optimism, urging individuals to be creative, question convention, decry a "foolish consistency," and call institutions to account. In an address delivered in Boston early in 1844, over a year before Polk took office, he called on the Young American "to obey your heart, and be the nobility of this land." Guided by what he called a "sublime and friendly Destiny," the United States was the "country of the Future...a country of beginnings, of projects, of vast designs, and expectations." Free of the inhibiting bonds of tradition, Americans may "inspire and express the most expansive and humane spirit," and speak for all the human race. "The bountiful continent is ours," he reminded his audience, "state on state, and territory on territory, to the waves of the Pacific sea."[2]

Few Americans matched the soaring rhetoric of New York journalist John Louis O'Sullivan, whose *Democratic Review* became a guiding light of romantic nationalism. "We are the nation of human progress," he wrote in 1839, "and who will, what can, set limits to our onward march?" Pointing to the "everlasting truth" of America's founding document, the Declaration of Independence, O'Sullivan found providential sanction in an American mission. "The far-reaching, the boundless future will be the era of American greatness," he declared. The United States, he believed was "destined to manifest to mankind the excellence of divine principles...to establish on earth the moral dignity and salvation of man" and the "immutable truth and beneficence of God." A large order for a young nation, but America in the minds of these spokesmen was unique, without a past to impede its progress, with only a future to define it. Six years later, O'Sullivan provided a label for his belief when he rearranged his words "destined to manifest" to the words "manifest destiny."[3]

In language laced with hyperbole, popular expressions of America's romantic nationalism flowed from the pens of writers and poets, of clergymen and humanitarian reformers, and of politicians. Rejecting all limits and expressing impatience with restraints on human endeavor, they believed that nothing lay beyond the grasp of individuals. Progress, salvation, even perfection became a matter of individual will. Emotion and intuition displaced the confining cold rationalism of earlier times. Trust your hearts, advised the romantics, not your heads. "There is a *spirit in man*," declared the historian George Bancroft, "which is the guide to truth."[4]

What was true of individuals was also true of nations. It was "an astonishing age," and it belonged to the United States. "In the few short years of its existence," one writer exclaimed, the country had "accomplished the work of ages." Technological discoveries, mind-boggling in their impact, had issued, one after another, from the nation's inventive genius. The railroad and the magnetic telegraph annihilated both distance and time. "We travel by steam and converse by lightning," it was said. "Railroad iron," Emerson boasted, "is a magician's rod, in its power to evoke the sleeping energies of land and water."[5]

It was an Age of Movement, declared the influential newspaper editor Horace Greeley, when to stand still was to fall behind. The locomotive became a metaphor for the nation. America was a "go a-head" country, and Americans were a "go a-head" people. "Go a-head" became a national motto, both intriguing and puzzling to Charles Dickens who sought to fathom its meaning during his visit to the United States in 1842. Any person who travels on anything slower than a locomotive, one political leader solemnly announced, cannot keep pace with the spirit of the age.[6]

Foreign travelers to the United States during the 1830s and 1840s were particularly annoyed by the bluster and brag they encountered in their journeys, in the railroad cars, at the country inns and eating establishments, and in the metropolitan hotels. As a people, they said, Americans were impetuous beyond any other, a characteristic they attributed to their "wonderful growth," their prosperity, and the

James K. Polk (1795-1849), from an engraving published by Rice and Buttre, about 1855. (Mexican War Graphics Collection, Special Collections Division, The University of Texas at Arlington Libraries, Arlington, Texas.)

"wild freedom" their institutions seemed to encourage. The language of the people, extravagant and exaggerated, was summed up in their creed: "There is nothing which we cannot do; few things we do not attempt; no heights that we are not sure to attain; no empires which we must not ultimately overthrow."[7]

By the mid-1840s, annoyance had turned into ridicule, especially among English writers who scoffed at what they called "ubiquitous qualities of the Universal Yankee nation." They took exception to claims that Zachary Taylor was a more brilliant military commander than Napoleon or Wellington. And they reacted with amazement to the claim that the march of Colonel Alexander Doniphan's Missouri volunteers across the deserts of northern Mexico surpassed the retreat of the ancient Greek army under Xenophon from Persia. A London periodical had had enough. "The genuine Yankee," it contended, "would not be able to *repose* in Heaven itself if he could travel further westward. He *must* go a-head." When Alexander Mackay toured the United States during the war, he observed the debates in the House of Representatives, where he listened in amazement to a congressman quoting from the Book of Genesis to prove the American claim to the whole of Oregon.

British reactions to the war with Mexico, especially in its early stages, often assumed the language of derision and scorn. Americans were indignant at the British historian Archibald Alison's contemptuous dismissal of the United States Army as both inadequate and insufficient to carry on a war with Mexico. With a force that was hardly equivalent to a Roman legion and only one-fifth the size of Bavaria's army, composed in large part of poorly trained, inexperienced backwoods militia, Alison predicted the United States would encounter only disaster in a contest with Mexico.[8]

Such attacks were answered in kind by American writers, whose new heights of verbosity were often mixed with a caustic Anglophobia. Walt Whitman, editor of a Brooklyn newspaper, shrugged off the slurs that were directed against "Yankeedoodle-dom" as but another demonstration of Britain's "spiteful meanness." "Let the Old World wag on under its cumbrous load of form and conservatism," Whitman wrote, "we are of a newer, fresher race and land."[9]

"A newer, fresher race and land." Whitman's words had a special resonance in the America of the mid-1840s. The youth and vitality of the United States were repeatedly dramatized by a contrast with declining and decadent Europe, where princes and monarchs stifled the democratic aspirations of the people. No contrast was drawn in more graphic terms than that of the traveler who had just returned from a European tour. "Europe is antiquated, decrepit, tottering on the verge of dissolution," he told his fellow-Americans. "The choicest products of her classic soil consist in relics, which remain as sad memorials of departed glory and fallen greatness! They bring up the memories of the dead, but inspire no hope for the living! Here everything is fresh, blooming, expanding and advancing."[10]

The United States, Americans were reminded at every turn, was a new nation, born of revolution and dedicated to the ideals of its founding charter. "New-born, free, healthful, [and] strong," as one writer put it, America had severed its ties not only with an out-worn past but also with the out-moded systems of Europe's absolutist monarchies, and had embarked on a unique experiment in democratic government with all the vigor, self-assurance and energy of youth. A new epoch had opened, and some argued that a new time-scale was in order. Notions of destiny and a heaven-favored mission filled the columns of the public prints. Young Americans were admonished to be "true to their trust," their task, according to a prospectus for "America in 1846," to "extend to all the people of the American continent...institutions based upon the light of reason and truth, upon the benefits and inherent and equal rights of all men."[11]

Young America became a popular slogan, and tributes to the Young American became subject-matter for poets and essayists. To a number of the country's literati, Young America was also more than a popular catch phrase. Imbued with the currents of an American romanticism, they sought to create a national literature that spoke to the heart, a literature for the people that breathed the spirit of democracy and reflected the uniqueness of America's role in the world—in other words, a distinctively American literature that would be in keeping with the ideals and aspirations of Young America.[12]

In December 1845, Edwin DeLeon, southern editor and self-styled "scion of this Young America," published an address entitled "The Position and Duties of 'Young America'" that provided the concept with a philosophical basis. There was nothing very original in his statement but because it appeared at a time when popular thought was particularly receptive, DeLeon has been credited with launching a movement, a role not unlike that of John L. O'Sullivan who first used the phrase manifest destiny during the same year.

"Nations," wrote DeLeon, "like men, have their seasons of infancy, manly vigor, and decrepitude." The United States, the "young Giant of the West," stood "in the full flush of exulting manhood, and the worn-out Powers of the Old World may not hope either to restrain or impede his onward progress." In advancing what has been called the organic theory of nationhood, DeLeon was reiterating a significant element in popular romantic thought. The notion that growth and development—organic change—applied to nations as well as to individuals, and, therefore, that each nation developed its own unique personality (often called a "national genius") became one of Young America's core beliefs.

DeLeon spoke at a time of increasing tension and fear of war: with Great Britain over the Oregon boundary question, a matter of considerable concern; and with Mexico over Texas annexation, a matter of lesser concern. Whether it be in Texas or in Oregon, wherever the extension of the area of freedom might take the United States, DeLeon added, let us be prepared to guard it against the "profaning foot of any foreign foe."[13]

A major portion of DeLeon's address was devoted to a strong call for a national literature, which by the mid-'40s had become the most urgent task of Young America. A nation, he insisted, was known by the literature it produces, and it was about time that Americans broke their literary dependence upon Great Britain. He lauded those figures who were leading the way: Washington Irving, whom he called the pioneer of "Young America"; the historian George Bancroft; and such writers of fiction as James Fenimore Cooper and William Gilmore

Simms. What the nation needed, he repeated, was a "youthful literature" that was as young and vigorous as the United States itself.

The resources for a national literature, DeLeon pointed out, were
at hand, waiting to be tapped by the talented and imaginative writer.
"What country," he urged, "ever yet possessed richer materials for
History, Eloquence, Poetry and Song, than ours?" The story of the settlement of the American colonies, he suggested, formed a "National
Epic on the grandest scale." American writers, moreover, must look
beyond the nation's borders, to Mexico and Central America, for
example, where a "rich mine of literary ore" lay buried among the sep-
ulchers and monuments of their ancient civilizations.[14]

To DeLeon, the United States was coming of age, moving into
manhood at a time when the lives of Americans were changing dra-
matically in a host of different ways spurred on by the rise of an indus-
trial establishment, technological improvements in transportation
and communication, the growth of cities and an increasing flow of
immigrants from Europe. At the same time, Americans were indeed
reaching out beyond their borders. An expanding commerce, an
increase in travel made possible by steam power on land and sea and
a heightened interest in exploration were carrying Americans to the
far corners of the globe. Clipper ships were regularly carrying goods
back and forth between the country's eastern port cities and those of
China, while large bulky wagons lumbering to northern Mexico
turned the Santa Fe trail into a busy highway. Fur traders roamed the
northern and central Rocky Mountains, penetrating the Pacific
Northwest and California, and a flourishing coastal trade brought
New England merchants to California's shores. Whaling vessels from
northeastern ports were carrying the United States flag into the
Pacific and Indian Oceans.

Government-sponsored expeditions were advancing knowledge of
the world's remote areas and demonstrating that the republic had the
will and the resources to carry out a vigorous extension of its influence. Naval expeditions to the Oregon country, the Amazon Basin,
Paraguay, western Africa, and the Near East, and the overland expeditions of John C. Frémont expanded the horizons of Americans while

stirring their romantic interest in nature, landscape and native peo-ples. The most ambitious effort was the United States Exploring Expedition, which left the United States in 1838 and returned four years later after surveying and mapping the west coast of South America, California, the Pacific Northwest, the islands of the south-west Pacific, and the waters of Antarctica. The immense collection of natural history specimens gathered by the expedition were placed on exhibit in Washington, later to be deposited with the new Smithsonian Institution. The five-volume narrative of the expedi-tion, promising descriptions of "Remote and hitherto Undiscovered Localities" and "Strange and Savage Races," was published in 1845 and widely read in subsequent years.[15]

At that moment, thousands of Americans were making the long trek overland to new homes in the lush western valleys of Oregon, where they immediately called for the extension of United States laws and institutions. Hundreds more were on their way to California. By 1846, the American population in Oregon exceeded 9000; as many as 500 American farmers called California home. The numbers would continue to increase.

Little wonder then that the United States was widely regarded as a "go a-head" nation, and its people as a "go a-head" people. Little wonder that the time had been dubbed an "age of movement." The United States at midcentury was still a nation in search of itself, a nation seeking a role and an identity in a rapidly changing world. Edwin DeLeon's Young America and its kindred expression, John L. O'Sullivan's manifest destiny, were popular manifestations of that search.

In 1845, the year both DeLeon and O'Sullivan issued their mani-festos, an effort was set in motion to define the nation by changing its name. The United States, by its very name, conjured a broad amor-phous entity, vast and full of variety. What was needed, it was thought, was a strong identification with place, with a geographic fea-ture. Early in the year, the New-York Historical Society appointed a three-man Committee on a National Name to recommend a new name that would more accurately identify the country. "What we want," the committee stated, "is a sign of our identity....We want a watchword more national than that of states." The committee chose Allegania, a decision that satisfied almost no one. Washington Irving, who had first suggested it, thought the name appropriate for it not only described an important geographic feature but it was also of indigenous Indian derivation. The word, he said, had "magic in it." A few agreed, pointing out that the country was indebted to the Alleghany range "for a great part of its beauty and healthfulness."

The effort, as one might expect, inspired a flurry of other suggestions, some of them ludicrous. Edgar Allan Poe preferred the "sonorous, more liquid" Appalachia to the "gutteral" Allegania. Another proposed the Republic of Washington. A Boston editor thought Yankeedonia or Yankeedum might do. In the end, the effort was abandoned for lack of support. Most agreed that the name United States of America, forged in the furnace of revolution by the founding fathers, be retained as the nation's official designation, while the generally accepted terms America and Americans continue to refer to the country and its people. The latter nomenclature by the 1840s was in common usage, not only in the United States but overseas as well. "The world over," one individual observed, "we are designated as 'Americans.'"[16]

The war with Mexico was the first major national crisis faced by Americans during this period of unprecedented social and economic change, and it immediately became a significant element in the effort to define a role for the young republic. Whether we call it romantic nationalism or the spirit of the age, Young America or manifest destiny and mission, the popular feeling was critical to the country's growth and development. Beneath all the exaggerated rhetoric that it generated were ideas of substance that exerted a profound and powerful influence on the shaping of the nation. They provided the backdrop before which the drama of the war with Mexico was played out.

In 1848, as Americans awaited news of Mexico's ratification of the peace treaty, thoughts turned toward the need for a history of the war. The would-be historian was cautioned to give due attention to the spirit that lay behind the facts. Those who believe "that the *facts* of history are given when every statement is made out with accuracy," mistake the nature of their task, for the "greatest fact of all is the feeling which originated the movement, and the enthusiasm which bore it onward."[17]

What was called "feeling," or what others called "spirit," was evident at the war's beginning in the response of young Americans to the call for volunteers. Many of those who responded were motivated by a thirst for adventure mixed with a sense of patriotic duty. They perceived themselves as travelers, as explorers and as pioneers (the "go a-head" volunteers), opening one more window through which Americans back home could view a remote and exotic clime, pushing back the horizons of knowledge, experiencing a strange and ancient land they had only dreamed of before, sharing their romantic fascination with alien manners and customs and with an antiquity that they could not find in their own country.

The "dare-devil war spirit" of the volunteer soldiers aroused the admiration of New England historian William Hickling Prescott, who had chronicled the sixteenth-century Spanish conquest of Mexico and who many thought would be the logical historian of the nineteenth-century American conquest. Although he opposed the war, Prescott saw in the volunteers the "pioneers of civilization," proof of the "indomitable energy" of the American people. "We go ahead," he wrote, in language that echoed those who saw in the war a coming of age. "We go ahead like a great lusty brat that will work his way into the full size of man."[18]

To Walt Whitman, America's fighting men also reflected the patriotism of the country's common people. The mass demonstrations that celebrated the victories in Mexico in city after city moved Whitman to declare that there was no more "admirable impulse in the human soul than *patriotism*." The large gatherings convinced him that the Mexican War was a great democratic mission. Although he argued that military superiority was not by itself a sign of national greatness, he believed that the triumphs on the battlefield would "elevate the *true* self-respect of the American people" to a point commensurate with "such a great nation as ours really is." Like many others, he found the roots of patriotism in the nation's revolutionary origins. The American Revolution was a continuing revolution, one without end that called for vigilance and sacrifice if midcentury Americans were to prove worthy of their past. Analogies were constantly drawn between the "spirit of '76" and the "spirit of '46," and the volunteers were as often admonished to show the world that the patriotism of the fathers could still be found in the hearts of the sons.[19]

The war touched American lives more intimately and with greater immediacy than any event to that time. Coinciding with the "print explosion" of the mid-nineteenth century, of which the penny press was but one manifestation, the war was reported in more detail than "any previous war in any part of the world." Fast steam presses, innovative techniques in news gathering, the employment of war correspondents for the first time (including many volunteers who reported the war for their home-town newspapers), the use of the new magnetic telegraph, and the rapid proliferation of books and periodicals, all combined to carry the war into people's lives on an unprecedented scale. The episodes of the war, the experiences of its combatants in camp and field, even the intentions and feelings of the enemy were "more thoroughly known by mankind, than those of any war that has ever taken place."[20]

The race to supply the public with accounts of the war began as soon as news of the first battles at Palo Alto and Resaca de la Palma appeared in the nation's press, and it continued unabated through most of the war. Writers were impatient, publishers were impatient, and, most important, the reading public was impatient. Publishers raced against time and their competitors to put their histories and biographies before the public, fearing that the war might end before they could reap the rewards of the war-spirit. Every soldier, it was said, fancied himself a historian of the war; some of the histories that appeared as soon as the fighting began were little more than collections of newspaper reports. The result was a veritable "Niagara of books," books "foaming with excitement" with pages that "blaze ever with *red*." Reviewers complained loudly of the flood that inundated their desks, protesting that they could barely keep up with the multitude of books generated by the war. No conflict, it seemed, had ever had so many chroniclers. The literature, complained an opponent of the war, "enters every nook and corner of the land."[21]

Some of Young America's spokesmen, encouraged by the effusion of printed material, hoped that the fighting would produce the great national literature they felt the country so badly needed. The war, they predicted, would form a distinct epoch in the history of American letters, for out of the contest would come all the elements of romance and drama, of heroism, sacrifice and patriotic devotion that writers would need for years to come. The war with Mexico, they hoped, would do for American literature what the Napoleonic wars were doing for English literature.

Among the first to respond to the challenge were the nation's poets. Hardly a month after the war began, a New York newspaper reported that a "poetical mania" was sweeping the land.[22] It was an age of poetry, when newspapers regularly featured original poems on their front pages, when new books of poetry were announced almost daily. Some would-be Homers— like William C. Falkner, a Mississippi volunteer and great-grandfather of the twentieth-century novelist— saw in the war a conflict of epic proportions, and they set themselves the task of providing Young America with its own *Iliad*. Three years after the war's end, Falkner published at his own expense his epic poem *The Siege of Monterey* in 493 stanzas, about 4000 lines, described by one recent critic as the "strangest poetical composition in the language." Others, less ambitious, decided that there was no need to create another *Iliad*, for the whole country was "engaged in acting an Epic."[23] More popular were those poems inspired by battles. There were so many poems entitled "Monterey" (as the name was often spelled by people in the United States) that it was difficult to keep them apart, but even Monterrey was soon eclipsed by Buena Vista. Abolitionists like John Greenleaf Whittier, James Russell Lowell, even William Lloyd Garrison himself, protested the war in poetic form, sometimes to good effect.

Those writers whose names have long been acknowledged as major figures in the remarkable flowering of American literature

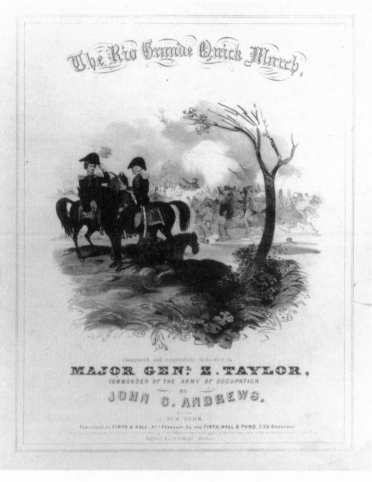

Sheet Music *The Rio Grande Quick March* by John G. Andrews. New York: Firth & Hall, 1846. (Mexican War Sheet Music Collection, Special Collections Division, The University of Texas at Arlington Libraries, Arlington, Texas.)

known as the American Renaissance were generally silent on the conflict. Herman Melville's only contribution was a series of unsigned comic articles satirizing Zachary Taylor that appeared in a humor magazine.[24] Nathaniel Hawthorne's response to the war was published four years later when he wrote a flattering biography of wartime brigadier-general and 1852 presidential candidate Franklin Pierce.[25] Emerson was ambivalent toward the war, opposing it on the one hand while on the other expressing admiration for the American people who, he said, were "fast opening their own destiny." Rejecting the war as a means for expanding the nation, Emerson believed that Americans, with their superior civilization, would "in the course of ages" overrun the continent peaceably.[26] Only James Fenimore Cooper, then in the last years of a distinguished and productive career, published a Mexican War novel: *Jack Tier; or, The Florida Reef*. A strong supporter of the United States Navy, Cooper was disappointed that the navy did not play a greater role in the fight. He made up for it by writing a novel of the war at sea, a fanciful fiction that had little impact.[27]

For all the outpouring of literary efforts, the war with Mexico did not meet the expectation that a great national literature would result. Indeed, many of Young America's leaders began to question whether wars in general truly inspire great literary effort. While many of the productions—especially the cheap paperbound Gothic romances with Mexican War settings—have value as both reflecting and shaping popular perceptions of the war, they hardly represented the national character and aspirations in the ways Young America expected.[28]

What did the end of the Mexican War mean to the American people? For one thing, as the *Democratic Review* suggested, it meant the "reduction of our enormous expenses by the withdrawal of the army, and the cessation with it of the excessive jobbing which has been so long going on." The war had cost the nation about 100 million dollars; its demands had resulted in a drain of specie to Mexico that had been only partially offset by unprecedented exports of American grain to Europe. The news of Mexico's ratification of the

peace treaty coincided with the opening of bids in Washington for a
new government loan, and the impact of the announcement that the
war had ended was immediately apparent. The entire new loan was
taken by American and British banking houses on terms that were
highly advantageous to the government. "Shrewd capitalists as the
large European bankers are," crowed the *New-York Tribune*, "they
must be convinced that this Government is no longer an experiment,
and that its bonds are as good security as those of any debt-ridden
State of Europe."[29]

Vast new territories had now become part of the United States,
although some Americans felt that these areas—the "impenetrable
mountains and dry narrow valleys" of California and the "trackless,
treeless...and utterly uninhabitable" New Mexico—would prove
useless to the country. Most of the new land, it was thought, would
become the haunt of savages and outlawed desperadoes, a drain on
the national treasury and a constant threat to the nation's frontier
settlements. Mexico, some believed, had forced a shrewd bargain,
ridding herself of her worthless territory and receiving fifteen million dollars from the United States for the sacrifice. One Whig
newspaper complained that "it cannot be seriously urged that the
distant deserts which Mexico grants us, are any equivalent for the
money she receives."[30]

Americans quickly assigned a significance to their triumph in
Mexico that reflected national pride. It was the country's first foreign
conflict, fought on foreign soil far from the centers of population. The
vast area covered by the military campaigns and the difficult terrain
over which much of the fighting took place had raised serious problems
for supply, communication and transportation. For the first time, the
nation was obliged to raise, train and equip large numbers of volunteer
troops, and to move the troops quickly to the areas of military operation. The efficiency with which these problems were met seemed to
demonstrate the energy and strength of the young republic.

Some critics now conceded that the war had shown "that a people
...devoted to the arts of peace, possessing free political institutions,
can vanquish a military people, governed by military despots." The

war, many agreed, had won new respect for the "model republic" and had convincingly refuted those who had argued that republics, lacking a powerful centralized government, could not successfully wage a foreign war. The language of contempt so often voiced by Europeans, wrote New York's wealthy Whig merchant Philip Hone, "is heard no more; the little foibles of Brother Jonathan are forgotten in contemplation of his indomitable courage."[31]

For Young Americans, the war with Mexico marked the advance of the United States from youth into manhood. "The young Giant of the West" now stood forth "in the full flush of exulting manhood," while still retaining the enthusiasm, the boldness and the enterprise of youth. The war, according to historian Nathan Covington Brooks, displayed to the world "a majestic power and energy, a youthful freshness of spirit combined with a manly vigour." Even critics hailed the new blend of manhood with "the ardor and activity of youth." It was a theme that was echoed in the popular print. "The nation," wrote Cooper, had passed "from the gristle into the bone."[32]

The transition seemed complete when, in mid-March 1848, about six weeks after the peace treaty had been signed and less than two weeks after its ratification by the United States Senate, news reached New York of a revolution in France, the abdication of the French King, and the proclamation of a French Republic. The news sent shock waves throughout the country. Mass demonstrations were held in the cities at which editors, orators and politicians sounded the death knell of monarchical absolutism. *La Marseillaise* was played and sung, shops displayed the French tricolor, and men wore liberty caps.

The role of the United States was unmistakable. "This republic," declared the *New York Herald*, "is the model and exemplar of the revolutionists in France, and all of Europe." With the victorious war with Mexico just ended, commented another paper, "we possess one of the highest characters in the world, at this time." The new prestige and respect gained from the war had propelled the United States into a position of leadership in the "history of civilization and the human race." The French revolution, it was widely assumed, was an unexpected consequence of the war with Mexico. To George Wilkins

Kendall, correspondent in Mexico during the war and now relaying dispatches to his newspaper from Paris, it seemed especially appropriate that the anniversary of the battle of Palo Alto should be observed in the French capital.[33]

On July 4, 1848, the long-awaited ratification of the treaty by the Mexican congress arrived at the White House, the same day that the cornerstone of the Washington Monument was dedicated—an auspicious coincidence. The dedication address was delivered by Robert C. Winthrop, leader of the Whig party, Massachusetts congressman and speaker of the House of Representatives. The day, he noted, not only commemorated the achievement of American independence but also marked "the precise epoch at which we have arrived in the world's history." A war against a foreign foe had just been won, and he paid tribute to the "veterans of the line and the volunteers" who stood before him. Winthrop pointed to the revolutions at that moment convulsing Europe, popular uprisings in which the "influence of our own institutions" and the "results of our own example" could be seen. "The great doctrines of our own Revolution," he said, "are proclaimed as emphatically this day in Paris, as they were seventy-two years ago this day in Philadelphia."

Finally, Winthrop invoked the language of Young America. The "great American-built locomotive, 'Liberty,'" he declared, still held its course, "on the track of human freedom, unimpeded and unimpaired; gathering strength as it goes; developing new energies to meet new exigencies," with a speed that "knows no parallel."[34]

NOTES

1. James K. Polk, "Inaugural Address, March 4, 1845," James D. Richardson, comp., *Messages and Papers of the Presidents, 1789-1897*, 10 vols. (Washington, 1897), vol. 4, pp. 373-82 (quotations, pp. 373-76).

2. Ralph Waldo Emerson, "The Young American," *Dial*, vol. 4 (April 1844), pp. 484-507, reprinted in Robert W. Johannsen, ed., *Democracy on Trial* (2d. edition, Urbana: University of Illinois Press, 1988), pp. 4-18 (quotations, pp. 15, 10, 7).

3. John L. O'Sullivan, "The Great Nation of Futurity," *Democratic Review*, vol. 6 (November 1839), pp. 426-30. For his first use of the phrase manifest destiny, see "Annexation," *Democratic Review*, vol. 17 (July and August 1845), p. 5.

4. George Bancroft, "The Office of the People in Art, Government and Religion," *Literary and Historical Miscellanies* (New York: Harper and Brothers, 1855), pp. 408-35, reprinted in Joseph L. Blau, ed., *Social Theories of Jacksonian Democracy* (New York: Liberal Arts Press, 1954), pp. 263-73 (quotation, p. 263).

5. Richard S. Fisher, *The Book of the World*, 2 vols. (New York: J.H. Colton, 1850), vol. 1, p. 109; Alexander Doniphan, in *Addresses . . . Before the Officers and Cadets of the United States Military Academy* (New York: Burroughs, 1848), p. 18; Emerson, "The Young American," in Johannsen, *Democracy on Trial*, p. 7.

6. Horace Greeley, "The Age We Live In," *Nineteenth Century*, vol. 1 (1848), p. 54; Stephen A. Douglas, quoted in Robert W. Johannsen, "Stephen A. Douglas and the American Mission," *The Frontier, The Union, and Stephen A. Douglas* (Urbana: University of Illinois Press, 1989), p. 92.

7. *Southern Quarterly Review*, vol. 14 (October 1848), pp. 511-12.

8. *Literary World*, vol. 5 (September 1, 1849), pp. 181-82, quoting the London *Athenaeum*, No. 1134 (June 21, 1849), p. 736; Alexander Mackay, *The Western World; or, Travels in the United States in 1846-47*, 3 vols. (London: R. Bentley, 1849), vol. 1, p. 301; Archibald Alison, *History of Europe from the Commencement of the French Revolution ... to the Restoration of the Bourbons*, 7th ed., 20 vols. (Edinburgh and London: W. Blackwood and sons, 1848), vol. 19, pp. 39-40.

9. Walt Whitman, *The Gathering of the Forces*, Cleveland Rodgers and John Black, eds., 2 vols. (New York: G.P. Putnam's Sons, 1920), vol. 1, pp. 46-47, 32-33.

10. Stephen A. Douglas, *Congressional Globe*, 32 Congress, 2 Session, Appendix, p. 273 (March 16, 1853).

11. Emerson, "The Young American," in Johannsen, *Democracy on Trial*, p. 10; "America in 1846. The Past—The Future," *Democratic Review*, vol. 18 (January 1846), pp. 57-64 (quotation, p. 64).

12. John Stafford, *The Literary Criticism of "Young America": A Study in the Relationship of Politics and Literature, 1837-1850* (Berkeley: University of California Press, 1952), pp. 82-94. See also two articles in the *Democratic Review*: "Nationality in Literature," vol. 20 (March 1847), pp. 264-72; and "Nationality in Literature," vol. 20 (April 1847), pp. 316-20.

13. Edwin DeLeon, *The Position and Duties of "Young America," An Address Delivered Before the Two Literary Societies of the South Carolina College, December, 1845* (Columbia, South Carolina: A.S. Johnston, 1845), p. 25. For more on "organic nationalism," see Merle Curti, "Young America," *American Historical Review*, vol. 32 (October 1926), pp. 34-55; and Merle Curti, *The Roots of American Loyalty* (New York: Columbia University Press, 1946), pp. 174 ff.

14. DeLeon, *Position and Duties of "Young America,"* p. 24.

15. Advertisement, *Democratic Review*, vol. 18 (May 1846), unnumbered page. The standard authority on the United States Exploring Expedition, its scientific contributions, and its role in gaining respect for the United States is William Stanton, *The Great United States Exploring Expedition of 1838-1842* (Berkeley: University of California Press, 1975).

16. Fred Somkin, *Unquiet Eagle: Memory and Desire in the Idea of American Freedom, 1815-1860* (Ithaca, New York: Cornell University Press, 1967), pp. 110-11; [Henry T. Tuckerman], "Alleghan, or Alleghanian America," *Democratic Review*, vol. 16 (May 1845), pp. 492-94; *Edgar Allan Poe*, in *Graham's Magazine*, vol. 29 (December 1846), p. 312; *Niles' National Register*, vol. 68 (April 12, 19, 1845), pp. 88, 99.

17. *American* [Whig] *Review*, vol. 7 (June 1848), p. 653.

18. Roger Wolcott, ed., *The Correspondence of William Hickling Prescott, 1833-1847* (Boston: Houghton Mifflin Company, 1925), pp. 648, 658, 629.

19. Whitman, *Gathering of the Forces*, vol. 1, pp. 82-85.

20. Frank Luther Mott, *American Journalism: A History of Newspapers in the United States Through 250 Years, 1690 to 1940* (New York: MacMillan Company, 1941), pp. 248-49; *Niles' National Register*, vol. 73 (September 25, 1847), p. 53.

21. John Frost, *The Mexican War and Its Warriors* (New Haven and Philadelphia: H. Mansfield, 1848), p. 120; *Literary World*, vol. 2 (September 4, 1847), p. 115; *Southern Literary Messenger*, vol. 21 (January 1855), p. 1; *Methodist Quarterly Review*, vol. 30 (January 1848), pp. 84-85; Abiel Abbot Livermore, *The War with Mexico Reviewed* (Boston: American Peace Society, 1850), pp. 227, 229.

22. *New York Herald*, June 17, 1846.

23. Hilton Anderson, "Colonel Falkner's Preface to the *Siege of Monterey*," *Notes on Mississippi Writers*, vol. 3 (Spring 1970), pp. 36-40; *Literary World*, vol. 2 (September 11, 1847), p. 130.

24. Luther Stearns Mansfield, "Melville's Comic Articles on Zachary Taylor," *American Literature*, vol. 9 (January 1938), pp. 411-18.

25. Nathaniel Hawthorne, *Life of Franklin Pierce* (Boston: Reed and Fields, 1852); Lee H. Warner, "With Pierce, and Hawthorne, in Mexico," *Essex Institute Historical Collections*, vol. 111 (July 1975), pp. 213-20.

26. *Journals of Ralph Waldo Emerson*, William H. Gilman, *et al.*, eds., 14 vols. (Cambridge: Harvard University Press, 1960-78), vol. 9, pp. 74, 430-31; Emerson, "War," *Aesthetic Papers*, Elizabeth P. Peabody, ed. (Boston: The Editor, 1849), pp. 36-50. See also, John Q. Anderson, "Emerson on Texas and the Mexican War," *Western Humanities Review*, vol. 13 (Spring, 1959), pp. 191-99.

27. James Fenimore Cooper, *Jack Tier; or, The Florida Reef* (Mohawk ed., New York: Putnam's, 1896). See also Thomas Philbrick, *James Fenimore Cooper and the Development of American Sea Fiction* (Cambridge: Harvard University Press, 1961), pp. 203-09.

28. For more on the "paperback explosion," see Robert W. Johannsen, *To the Halls of the Montezumas: The Mexican War in the American Imagination* (New York: Oxford University Press, 1985), pp. 186-94.

29. *Democratic Review*, vol. 22 (May 1848), p. 472; Washington *National Intelligencer*, June 19, 1848; *Bankers' Magazine*, vol. 2 (March 1848), p. 576; *New-York Tribune*, March 7, 1848.

30. *New-York Tribune*, February 26, 1848; Washington *National Intelligencer*, July 7, 1848.

31. [Hunt's] *Merchants' Magazine*, vol. 18 (April 1848), p. 463; *The Diary of Philip Hone, 1828-1851*, Allan Nevins, ed. (New York: Dodd, Meade and Company, 1936), p. 869.

32. DeLeon, *The Position and Duties of "Young America,"* p. 25; Nathan Covington Brooks, *Complete History of the Mexican War* (Philadelphia: Grigg, Elliot, 1849), p. 539; *The Diary of Philip Hone*, p. 869; Cooper, "Introduction," *The Spy: A Tale of the Neutral Ground* (New York: George P. Putnam, 1849), pp. vii-viii.

33. *New York Herald*, March 19, 20, 21, 25, 30, April 11, 1848; *Littell's Living Age*, vol. 18 (July 29, 1848), p. 238.

34. Robert C. Winthrop, "National Monument to Washington. An Oration Delivered at the Seat of Government, on the Occasion of Laying the Corner-Stone of the National Monument to Washington, July 4, 1848," in *Washington, Bowdoin, and Franklin as Portrayed in Occasional Addresses* (Boston: Little, Brown and Company, 1876), pp. 9-28.

Selected Readings and Viewing

Bauer, Jack. *The Mexican War*. Lincoln: University of Nebraska Press, 1974.

Beck, Warren. *Historical Atlas of the American West*. Norman: University of Oklahoma Press, 1989.

Beck, Warren and Ynez Haase. *Historical Atlas of New Mexico*. Norman: University of Oklahoma Press, 1969.

Benjamin, Thomas. "Recent Historiography of the Origins of the Mexican War." *New Mexico Historical Review*, Vol. 54, No. 3 (1979), pp. 169-181.

Calderon de la Barca, Frances. *Life in Mexico*. London: Dent, 1973.

Chamberlain, Samuel. *My Confession: The Recollections of a Rogue*. Lincoln: University of Nebraska Press, 1987.

Connor, Seymore and Odie Faulk. *North America Divided: The Mexican War, 1846-1848*. New York: Oxford University Press, 1971.

Costeloe, Michael P. *The Central Republic in Mexico, 1835-1846*. New York: Cambridge University Press, 1993.

Description of the Republic of Mexico; Including its Physical and Moral Features, Geography, Agriculture, Products, Manufactures, etc. Illustrated by a map, in which is included smaller maps of the Valley

of Mexico, and the fields of Palo Alto, and Resaca de la Palma.
Philadelphia: Thomas Cowperthwait & Co., 1846.

Eisenhower, John. *So Far From God: The U.S. War with Mexico,*
1846-1848. New York: Random House, 1989.

Ewing, Russell C., ed. *Six Faces of Mexico: History, People, Geography,*
Government, Economy, Literature and Art. Tucson: University of
Arizona Press, 1966.

Farnham, Thomas Jefferson. *Mexico: Its Geography, its People, and its*
Institutions with a map containing the result of the latest explorations
of Fremont, Wilkes, and others. New York: H. Long and Brother,
1846.

Faulk, Odie B. and Joseph A. Stout, eds. *The Mexican War: Changing*
Interpretations. Chicago: Sage Press, 1973.

Frazier, Donald S., ed. *The United States and Mexico at War:*
Nineteenth-Century Expansionism and Conflict. New York: Simon
& Schuster Macmillan, 1998.

Halls of the Montezumas; or Mexico, in Ancient and Modern Times;
Containing a…History of the Ancient and Modern Races,
Antiquities, and especially its splendid Palaces and Halls of State; also
its Geography, Government, Institutions, Mines, Minerals and
Churches…with the Conquest by Cortes and a Sketch of the late
War with the United States, including the Treaty of Peace. New York:
J. C. Burdick, 1848.

Haynes, Sam W. *James K. Polk and the Expansionist Impulse.* New
York: Longman, 1997.

Herrera Serna, Laura, ed. *México en guerra (1846-1848): Perspectivas*
regionales. Mexico City: Consejo Nacional para la Cultura y las
Artes, 1997.

Jackson, Jack. "General Taylor's 'Astonishing' Map of Northeastern
Mexico" *Southwestern Historical Quarterly,* Vol. 101, No. 2
(October, 1997), pp. 143-173.

Johannsen, Robert W. *To the Halls of the Montezumas: The Mexican War in the American Imagination*. New York: Oxford University Press, 1985.

Lander, Ernest M., Jr. *The Reluctant Imperialists: Calhoun, The South Carolinians, and the Mexican War* (Baton Rouge: Louisiana State University Press, 1980).

Lavender, David. *Climax at Buena Vista: The American Campaigns in Northeastern Mexico, 1846-1847*. Philadelphia: J.B. Lippincott, 1966.

Naufal, Victor M. Ruiz, Ernesto Lemoine, and Arturo Gálvez Medrano. *El Territorio Mexicano* (Vol. 1, "La Nación"; Vol. 2, "Los Estados"; and folio, "Planos y Mapas"). Mexico: Instituto Mexicano del Seguro Social, 1982.

Pitt, Leonard. *The Decline of the Californios*. Berkeley: University of California Press, 1971.

Pletcher, David. *The Diplomacy of Annexation: Texas, Oregon, and the Mexican War*. Columbia: University of Missouri Press, 1973.

Price, Glenn W. *Origins of the War with Mexico: The Polk-Stockton Intrigue*. Austin: University of Texas Press, 1967.

Rebert, Paula. "Mapping the United States-Mexico Boundary: Cooperation and Controversy." *Terrae Incognitae—The Journal for the History of Discoveries*, Vol. 28 (1996), pp. 58-71.

Reed, Nelson. *The Caste War of Yucatán*. Stanford: Stanford University Press, 1964.

Reina, Leticia. "The Sierra Gorda Peasant Rebellion, 1847-50" in Friedrich Katz, *Riot, Rebellion, and Revolution*. Princeton: Princeton University Press, 1988, pp. 269-294.

Richmond, Douglas W. "Yucatán's Struggle for Sovereignty During the Mexican-U.S. Conflict, 1836-1848." In Richard Sanchez, Eric Van Young, and Gisela Von Wobeser, eds. *La ciudad y el campo en la historia de México*. Mexico City: Instituto de

Investigaciones Históricas, Universidad Autónoma de México, 1992, pp. 173-183.

_____. ed. *Essays on the Mexican War*. College Station: Texas A&M University Press, 1986.

Santoni, Pedro. "A Fear of the People: The Civic Militia of Mexico in 1845." *Hispanic American Historical Review*, Vol. 65, No. 2 (May 1988), pp. 269-288.

_____. *Mexicans at Arms: Puro Federalists and the Politics of War, 1845-1848*. Fort Worth: Texas Christian University Press, 1996.

Smith, Justin H. *The War with Mexico*. 2 vols. New York: The McMillan Company, 1919.

The U.S.-Mexican War, video series produce by KERA and PBS, 1998. (4 hours).

Van Young, Eric, ed. *Mexico's Regions: A Comparative History and Development*. San Diego: Center for U.S.-Mexican Studies, the University of California, 1992.

Velasco Márquez, Jesús. *La guerra del 47 y la opinión pública (1845-1848)*. Mexico City: Secretaría de Educación Pública, 1975.

Walker, Henry P. and Don Bufkin. *Historical Atlas of Arizona*. Norman: University of Oklahoma Press, 1979.

Weber, David. *The Mexican Frontier, 1821-1846: The American Southwest under Mexico*. Albuquerque: University of New Mexico Press, 1982.

Weems, John Edward. *To Conquer a Peace: The War Between the United States and Mexico*. College Station: Texas A&M University Press, 1974.

West, Robert Cooper. *Sonora: Its Geographical Personality*. Austin: The University of Texas Press, 1993.

West, Robert and John Augelli. *Middle America: Its Lands and Peoples*. Englewood Cliffs, New Jersey: Prentice Hall, 1966.

Winders, Richard Bruce. Mr. *Polk's Army: The American Military Experience in the Mexican War.* College Station: Texas A&M University Press, 1997.

Zoraida Vázquez, Josefina, ed. *De la rebelión de Texas a la guerra del 47.* Mexico City: Nueva Imagen, 1994.

_____, ed. *La fundación del estado mexicano, 1821-1855.* Mexico City: Nueva Imagen, 1994.

_____, ed. *México al tiempo de su guerra con Estados Unidos (1846-1848).* Mexico City: Fondo de Cultura Económica, 1997.

The Contributors

Richard Francaviglia is a historian and geographer whose studies focus on the Western United States. He is currently Professor of History and Director of the Center for Greater Southwestern Studies and the History of Cartography at The University of Texas at Arlington.

Miguel González Quiroga currently serves as a legislator to the state of Nuevo León, Mexico. After his term of office expires, he will return to teach at the Universidad Autónoma de Nuevo León in Monterrey, Mexico.

Sam W. Haynes is a historian specializing in early nineteenth century United States history. He is Associate Professor of History at The University of Texas at Arlington.

Robert W. Johannsen is widely published in the area of nineteenth century United States history. He is J. G. Randall Distinguished Professor of History Emeritus at the University of Illinois at Urbana-Champaign.

Douglas W. Richmond is a historian of Mexico and Latin America. He is Professor of History at The University of Texas at Arlington.

Mitchel Roth is a historian who has two major areas of interest—the western United States and the history of crime and punishment. He is Associate Professor of Criminal Justice at Sam Houston State University in Huntsville, Texas.

Richard Bruce Winders serves as Curator at the Alamo in San Antonio, and is a specialist in military aspects of the United States-Mexico war.

Josefina Zoraida Vázquez is widely recognized as a major authority on United States-Mexican relations. She is Professor of History at El Colegio de México in Mexico City.

Index